"The unique combination of experience, insight, humor, and history Jack Valenti brings to *Speak Up with Confidence* makes it not only an enjoyable read, but an invaluable tool. *Speak Up with Confidence* remains the essential primer for everyone who is called upon to speak in public."
— TOM DASCHLE, MAJORITY LEADER, UNITED STATES SENATE

"To write a book about public speaking is one thing, to actually deliver is another. I have had the joy of listening to Jack Valenti speak on several occasions. He is the best public speaker I have ever heard. *Speak Up with Confidence* is the Bible on public speaking."
— MICHAEL DOUGLAS

"Jack Valenti offers solid advice and wisdom on the arts of public speaking. This new edition is especially timely, and it deserves to be widely read."
— TED KENNEDY, UNITED STATES SENATE

"I've been listening to Jack Valenti speak for years, and I can honestly say that few people do it better. He knows how to capture—and convince—a tough audience. Full of the insight Jack has gained from years of experience, *Speak Up with Confidence* is an invaluable book for all."
— SUMNER M. REDSTONE, CHAIRMAN AND CEO, VIACOM

"Jack Valenti holds a room because he knows what he's talking about. Read *Speak Up with Confidence*. He also knows what he's writing about."
— WARREN BEATTY

"*Speak Up with Confidence* is a masterfully crafted guide to public speaking. In simple yet eloquent language, Jack Valenti leads the reader through the all-important steps for developing and delivering a speech with aplomb and authority."
— WILLIAM S. COHEN, FORMER SECRETARY OF DEFENSE AND CHAIRMAN AND CEO, THE COHEN GROUP

Speak Up with Confidence

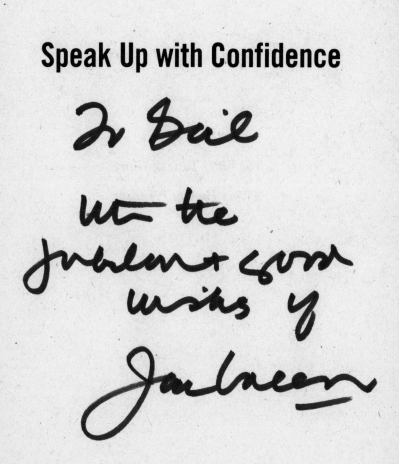

To Gail

With the
Jubilant good
wishes of

Jack Valenti

Speak Up with
Confidence

How to Prepare, Learn, and
Deliver Effective Speeches

Jack Valenti

HYPERION

NEW YORK

Contents

vii

Acknowledgments

TO BOB MILLER, high chieftain of Hyperion, and Bob Iger, president of The Walt Disney Company, I say "thank you" for wise counsel and affectionate support.

I embrace my editor, Jennifer Lang, with great delight. Her lively intelligence, her never-failing "story-sense" and persistent encouragement kept me on an ascending curve of diligence. She was indispensable.

To my lawyer-agent-counselor, Robert Barnett, I offer my deepest gratitude. He never faltered in guiding me through the thickets, a rare guide indeed.

To my family, Mary Margaret, Courtenay, Pat, John and Alexandra, my wondrous gratitude for just being there for me, always.

Speak Up with Confidence

Introduction

ALL MY LIFE I have been fascinated with the art of public persuasion, or what most of us describe as "public speaking."

When I was ten years old I made my first speech in front of an audience. My father was pleased with my babblings at family gatherings and claimed that I had some talent for speaking. So one evening at a political rally in Houston, Texas, for the reelection of the current sheriff of Harris County, my father told me to say some nice words about the sheriff. He lifted me up on the speaker's rostrum (the rear of a flatbed truck) and the emcee put me on. I have no recollection of what I said that warm Houston evening, except I do remember the sheriff, T. A. Binford, a huge bulk of a man who ranged upward to six feet three. He wore shining brown cowboy boots and carried on his hips two pearl-handled .45s, slung low, just like those movie gunfighters in the Old West.

Introduction

If you were about to commit some naughty crime, you had best do it in some jurisdiction other than Harris County. You just didn't want to mess with Sheriff Binford. His method of operation was "Fire, Aim, Halt," in that order. The plain fact was, my father later confided, that Sheriff Binford was mighty pleased with my vocal endorsement. From that moment on, I found out that I truly enjoyed being on the speaker's rostrum.

As I became more absorbed in being a clinical observer of countless speeches, presentations, and TV panel shows, I thought, Why not put what I had learned and absorbed about public speaking on paper? Maybe others would find it of some modest use. The result was this book, *Speak Up with Confidence: How to Prepare, Learn, and Deliver Effective Speeches*. It seemed to engage the interest of enough people to make the book a brief best-seller. Over the years, I kept meeting people in airports, at public functions, who offered their gratitude for my book and told me how it helped them when they were called on to speak up at some gathering.

More importantly, the environment and landscape for public dialogue has changed. The TelePrompTer is now omnipresent—a staple at conventions, in television studios—whereas when my book first came out it had only sporadic influence. TV talk shows have proliferated. Panel discussions on television about science, economics, health, and civic enhancement have sprung up with the speed of rabbit warrens. More people are on their feet speaking at more conclaves in more cities and states than ever before.

Thus it is that I determined to bring *Speak Up with Confidence* up to the current moment, with new material, new observations, to give it new currency in a changing political, social, and cultural environment. However, the basic shape and form of preparing, learning, and delivering first-class public speeches and the labor required to achieve that goal remains the same.

Let us be clear: If you want to be able to rise before an audience, large or small, and speak to them so that they will listen to you, *you can do it*.

If you are a man or woman in business, college, in the professions; if you are interested in your community and choose to speak up from time to time to voice your concerns; if you are a public official or yearn to be one; if you are called upon to testify before Congress or your state legislature or your local city council, or your stockholders or employees; if you participate in civic clubs or other organizations—and you would like to become a competent public speaker, then this book is aimed at you. You can learn to speak better than you think possible.

I issue no guarantee that this book will teach you to become a great orator or a captivating speaker on TV. But I am very clearly and very specifically declaring that if you are willing to learn some simple rules, and apply those rules with personal discipline and concentrated work, you can achieve a level of professional competence in your speaking appearances that will lift your confidence and enthuse your spirit.

But there is a caveat. Nothing in this book will teach you anything unless you are willing to work hard. There is no magic word in this book. The magic comes from your own exertions, from the time, the discipline, and the commitment you put into the rules this book teaches you. Learning to speak well is no different from learning to ski or play the piano or rollerblade. You learn the basic rules, and then you practice. By the same token, you can't read this book and wake up in the morning a first-rate speaker.

Let me sum it up:

> *Learning to speak well demands work.*
> *Work is the pathway to achievement.*
> *Personal achievement will incite within you one of the most exciting emotions you can feel.*

If this formula is congenial to you, then read on. Soon, very soon, you will be able to speak up with confidence.

CHAPTER ONE

The Beginning

Why You Must Know What You Are
Going to Say

He approached the rostrum looking no less than
what he was, the commanding officer of one of the
largest corporations in America. Tall, tending a touch toward portliness, firm of jaw and thick of hair, he domi-
nated the others on the dais.

The audience, some thousand men and women in the
Waldorf Astoria ballroom, waited expectantly for the
words of a man they had been persuaded would offer
them wisdom beyond their means about the future of the
national economic landscape.

And then the blight began.

The corporate chief executive's thick, usually confident fingers clutched the sides of the speaker's lectern so
as not to betray their trembling. He cleared his throat,
and then, as a drowning man grabs a floating log, he
leaped into the text before him, eyes fastened on the type-

script, straining to keep jangling nerve ends from screech-
ing loud enough to be heard by all in the room. For much
of the speech all the audience saw was the top of his head.

The speech was a dud.

He droned when he should have talked. The confident,
imperious manner that served him so well in boardrooms
and staff meetings had fled. The speech he should have
read over and over again to know it cold had lain unre-
garded in his briefcase for too long.

In short, this fine figure of a powerful business executive failed the test that ought to be applied to the leader
of any enterprise: Can he stand before a group of people
and persuade them, inspire them, and finally convince
them?

It is a fact of life that too many people who ought to
have developed some facility in speaking have done no
such thing. How many public officials have you heard
who seem to have brought dullness and droning to a
high art?

If those who should speak well as part of their professional equipment can't do it, what about the vast majority of us who speak only occasionally? How can we be
expected to do even passably well?

There is nothing really special about speaking in public. It is not a gift genetically inherited, nor is it divinely
inspired. The truth is that speaking well before groups is
a learnable craft, just as woodworking, skiing, playing the
saxophone, ballroom dancing, gardening, sex, or roller-
skating are all learned.

The Beginning

Stage fright? It's nothing to be ashamed of. Even the most seasoned professionals are affected by it. Actors and actresses, who make their living by performing for others, are not immune to the clammy embrace of fear. Some great actors claim that fear is a stimulant, alerting the mind and the tongue, rousing the nerve centers to a fine sensitivity, tuned to the moment's duty. Total relaxation—fearlessness, if you will—can often be delusive, slackening the responses, loosening the very fibers that ought to be taut and ready. Stage fright, then, is a spur to achievement. It is a good sign, not a bad one.

I remember well an occasion when I appeared on an Academy Award television spectacular, to present the Best Foreign Picture award. My copresenter was the dazzlingly beautiful actress Jacqueline Bisset. Before we were to go on, she and I were stationed backstage waiting for our cue. We chatted aimlessly. At least she did. I was so intrigued by her, by her poise, her serene loveliness, and the graceful way she stood quietly, that I may have exposed my own nervousness, caused less by anticipation of our appearance on stage than by the fact that I was meeting and talking with her for the first time. As one does in moments like these, I resorted to small talk.

"It's interesting," I began, "that you will soon be visible to more people tonight than have seen all your movies, everywhere. There'll be about five hundred million people watching us tonight, here and around the world."

Her marvelously sculptured face suddenly grew taut. "My God," she exclaimed, "you shouldn't say things like that now. Five hundred million people!" The thought of that vast unseen populace struck her with noticeable impact. While the audience in the theater numbered some three thousand (a manageable group, I suspect, to an experienced actress) the possibility of fouling up lines before that terrifyingly large and surely attentive mass of viewers out there was a matter of more than casual concern. This was a "live" show—no second or third takes, but live—and that meant the first time was the only time.

Soon we were summoned to the edge of the back curtain by one of the assistant directors. "You'll go on next," he whispered. I nodded. Miss Bisset's smile was thin. Then we were being introduced, and we walked toward the Plexiglas rostrum from which protruded two long, slim microphones. The lights were intense, blotting out for a brief moment the seated audience, among whom were fabled personalities in motion pictures and television.

As we stood in our appointed places, I was to begin the dialogue. A bare second before I spoke, for some unaccountable reason I noticed her left hand resting on the lectern. It was trembling. Immediately I had the horrible thought that if this professional actress, so accustomed to performing before others, was in a state of—how shall I say—semi-fright, why on earth wasn't I? And, on the instant, I was.

But a heart-quiver later, the mysterious mechanism that pumps whatever it is that lubricates the mind, preparing words to slide effortlessly from their hiding places and burst forth in coherent speech, cranked up and I was speaking. It is also cheering to report that Miss Bisset never missed a beat. The professionalism that sustained her was in good working order and we finished our presentation, without fault and on time.

When we were done, I suddenly felt that inexpressible relief that comes to athletes, soldiers, performers, who have accomplished their assigned task in the face of threatened disaster. It was over and it had gone well. Miss Bisset, having overcome her momentary concern, was never more lovely.

I wondered about that event for some time.

I considered my own state of mind. Watching the trembling hand of Jacqueline Bisset could have thrown me off; it almost did. Why didn't it? The reason, I reflected, was quite simple: I was thoroughly prepared. I was confident that I knew what I was going to say, even though there is always the crutch of the TelePrompTer available to all who appear on the show.

It is no revelation to observant viewers of the Academy Award ceremonies that there is a huge electronic TelePrompTer beneath the lens of the camera positioned in the center of the auditorium. On this TelePrompTer each presenter's dialogue is printed in a size that even the most myopic would find hard to miss, giant white letters on a pure black background. The Academy Award producers, having small faith in the chancy nature of memory, provide this mnemonic safety net. Under the circumstances, the only way to flub one's dialogue is to be unable to read English or to forget to wear one's long-range glasses. That such mishaps have occurred on the Academy Award shows only certifies that if something can go wrong, it usually does. Particularly if one is negligent about preparation, or horror of horrors, if the Tele-PrompTer were to break down.

That same tableau was enacted on another Academy Award show, this time in 2001. My costar this time (why is it that I am so attracted to that billing?) was another extraordinary, graceful beauty, the celebrated French actress, Juliette Binoche. We were presenting the Best Foreign Language Film. On the Saturday rehearsal before the Sunday performance, we were taken through our entrance cues by the director. For some unfathomable reason we were to enter from backstage and then, in full audience view, we were supposed to mount a portable silver-colored staircase about three feet high and then descend the three feet down the other side onto the main stage. In our rehearsal, as we approached the small staircase I muttered aloud a sudden nightmare. "What would happen if I tripped on one of these steps and fell on my butt, dragging you down with me in front of a billion people?" Miss Binoche stiffened. There was for a fleeting moment a whisper of palpable unease that fluttered through her. I knew it wasn't the blight of falling on one's backside. It was the ultimate distress of doing it before a live audience and millions more watching on TV.

The Beginning

Came the big night and our big moment. We were introduced. She took my arm. The audience applauded. Suddenly we were confronted by the staircase. I gazed at the stairs with rising horror. Juliette's hand grasping my arm stiffened. This was stage fright in its finest grotesque form. I looked briefly at her, smiled the smile that said, We've gone up stairs a thousand times with no problems. So let's do it once more. She smiled. So it was that while my eyes never left my feet, I stepped up, as on my arm she glided in glorious harmony. We said our lines, I opened the envelope, and with a wide grin announced, "The Oscar goes to *Crouching Tiger, Hidden Dragon*," whereupon Ang Lee, the director, came bounding onto the stage to receive his coveted Oscar, the equivalent in the movie industry of the Nobel Prize.

The fact was that I knew my lines. I had practiced them a hundred times, particularly to get the correct pronunciation of Spanish, German, French names. I had them cold. Therefore I wasn't going to allow a few crummy stair steps to conquer me.

I had memorized my thirty-second speaking part on both Academy Awards. (Pitifully small, but then again, when five hundred million people out there are waiting for you to fall on your backside, thirty seconds can be an eternity.)

I had gone over the lines again, and again, and again, and again. I lost count of how many times I said those lines. I said them in the shower, as I was shaving, as I was sitting on an airplane. I could have said them backward (God, the horror of actually doing that). But the central fact was that I knew them, knew them cold, and the knowledge was like a warm embrace. It comforted me. It sustained me through the possibility of any untoward incident, even the trembling hand of a beautiful professional actress. If the TelePrompTer had blown a fuse, I could have danced through that blackout only because I was prepared for disaster.

The first, the foremost, the indispensable step, in making a speech—any kind of speech, whether it is a two-line introduction of another speaker, or a toast after dinner, or a formal presentation to a large convention, or a report to the Kiwanis Club on the state of the treasury, or the proposal of a budget for a board of directors—is to *know what you are going to say and know it cold*.

I have been on a number of Academy Award television shows and have been astonished on several occasions to see film pros stumble, even with the always-there Tele-PrompTer, and sometimes wander off into improvisations that curdled the blood of the show's director.

Why?

The explanation is simple: lack of preparation, casual

attention paid to essentials, failing to become thoroughly acquainted with what you are supposed to say.

If dedicated professionals can fall prey to this omission, then nonprofessionals must take special care. Getting ready for the speech is the first requirement. Without it, only the oratorical talented can survive. With it, every person who chooses to can be a satisfactory speaker.

Stage fright is an affliction that infects just about everyone who ever stands up to speak before an audience, including those you would think would be immune to it. Never was this more amply and astonishingly brought home to me than on the evening of November 21, 1963. I was living in Houston, the cofounder of an advertising agency, Weekley & Valenti. That night I was the chairman of a huge dinner honoring Houston's longtime congressman, Albert Thomas. The two main speakers were President John F. Kennedy and Vice President Lyndon Johnson. JFK and LBJ were on a swift visit to Texas, landing early that morning in San Antonio, now this evening in Houston, on to Ft. Worth early the next morning, with a noon stop in Dallas and then to Austin for a massive fund-raising dinner.

Just before the dinner began, the vice president asked me to join him backstage in a private curtained-off enclosure where sat LBJ and Mrs. Johnson, as well as the president and his glowingly beautiful wife. The vice president said, "Mr. President, this is Jack Valenti, who has been a big factor in your very successful visit to Houston. He's going on with me to Ft. Worth tomorrow and will be with us for the rest of the trip."

The president shook my hand, introduced me to his wife, and said: "Jack, I think I need to have you handle all my visits. I am grateful to you for all that you did to make Houston a big success." I stammered my thanks. Up close, JFK and Jacqueline Kennedy radiated glamour and charm. He was so at ease, without fear, so in command of the occasion. He was, in brief, presidential.

When the dinner speeches began, I was standing behind the dais, which was raised by some five feet above the floor. I was unseen by the audience, but I had an intimate view of the speakers. When the president was introduced, he came to the lectern, lean, handsome, and seemingly ready to find rapport with an audience that had literally gone wild with applause.

Then it was I saw it happen. The president's speech script lay before him. When he started speaking, I could not help watching his right hand. It was trembling, rapidly, ceaselessly. He put it on the lectern to lessen the tremors. As he spoke, his words, in the familiar JFK cadences, danced through the cavernous hall. But his hand was at his side again, trembling, trembling. I could not credit my eyes. This thoroughly confident leader, so much in authority, was infected with stage fright.

When he finished, the two thousand men and women in the audience vaulted to their feet, cheering and applauding. It was a triumphant experience. What it proved to me was that you can be assaulted by stage fright, as we all are, as even presidents are, and still impress on your audience all that you wanted to convey.

(The epilogue to JFK's Texas trip was a grotesque nightmare. It was an inexpressibly tragic piece of fate that sixteen hours later, in a senseless act of mindless malice, this gallant young man, thirty-fifth president of the United States, would be slain in the streets of Dallas. So this evening, November 21, 1963, that I met President Kennedy for the first time, was his last night on earth.)

Don't worry about stage fright. It'll keep your nerves at battle stations. And if you are prepared, you will, I promise you, get through the speech better than you ever thought possible even with stage fright.

Remember: You do not have to be a professional to make a good speech, but you do have to prepare. Very seldom will you be called on to speak without warning. If you have an assigned part on a program, know it in advance. You should also know the nature of your audience and your subject. Thus armed, anyone can learn to speak passably well and, more importantly, can continue to perfect his or her skills on an ever-ascending curve.

CHAPTER TWO

The Preparation

How to Be Ready to Say What You Want to Say

There are three methods of speaking:

1. From a prepared text.
2. With notes that give you an outline of what you have prepared to say.
3. Without notes. This is for the old pros, not for beginners. It is like trying to schuss down a steep ski slope the first time you put on skis. You will spend more time on your backside than you will skiing.

Let us begin with a prepared text. Later on we will pursue in some detail how to write a speech, but first we will concentrate on the preparation.

The first step is to have your speech typed *in exactly the form you will use when you deliver it.*

Do *not* practice a speech that has been put down on

paper in a form (that is, paragraphing and spacing) that is different from the reading copy you will use.

Break the speech up into paragraphs—short paragraphs. You will also find it useful to skip an extra line between paragraphs so that each may be seen as a separate, self-contained entity.

Read over your speech. Read it once, twice, three times—read it fifty times. Read it so often that it is almost committed to memory, though you need not go that far. And read it in the form that you will use when you rise to deliver the speech.

The trick is to read your speech so many times that the words are like old friends. You know them so well that each word is a familiar companion to you, not some alien shape that takes you by surprise. And each word you speak will immediately nudge you into recognizing the next word. Suddenly these old companions will be on your lips, formed easily and without fear.

If you have trouble pronouncing a specific word, take it out and insert another word that is more comfortable for you. There are some 500,000 words in the English language. Don't be afraid to edit, so that every word in the speech is one with which you feel at ease. Stumbling over a word or two sounds an alarm bell that alerts your audience to impending disaster. A mispronounced word, a word too ungainly for you to handle correctly, puts whatever follows in jeopardy. Avoid words with hissing sounds, or vowel and consonant juxtapositions that cause your tongue to become slovenly.

When I was in charge of President Lyndon Johnson's speech-writing staff, I pursued such words with the vigilance of a beagle on point. Whenever I wrote a speech for the president, I was overly cautious about using any word or name that had oral "thorns" in it. In editing and revising staff-written speeches, I went to extraordinary lengths to sniff out and excise such verbal briers. The president grew surly when we were going over a speech and he came across a word that some overliterate speech draftsman had inserted. He would invariably say, "What in the hell are you trying to do to me? Get that goddamn word out of there." The president, like so many of us, had difficulty with cumbersome words and words with foreign derivations. In particular I remember one speech that had the word "nuance," which LBJ brought forth as "new ants" (to the callous titters of the press). Terror is the only term adequate to describe my feelings when I recall that I failed to edit that word out of a presidential speech. That neglect later elicited one of the president's more awesome reactions in his appraisal of the author. I forget his exact words only because my conscience is easily outraged.

Read your speech over and over and over again. Read it until the words have become so settled in your mind you have no hesitancy in approaching each of them with easy familiarity.

After you have read the speech sufficiently to acquire this facility, next read the speech by paragraphs. Read the first paragraph again and again.

Then to the second paragraph. Again, the key words should carry you easily through the rest of the paragraph.

The same attention goes into the rest of the speech. Why? Why this drudging repetition?

Because you will soon make a strange, emancipating discovery. The mind is like a camera. It can photograph chunks of prose. If you have persistently aimed the camera of your eyes at each paragraph, the eye and the brain make an imprint of what you are reading. If you do this often enough, you can lift your gaze from the copy and almost see, in the retina of the eye, a positive reflection of what is on the paper. It is this "photographing" of each paragraph that will give you a special asset that separates good speakers from merely adequate or bad speakers. You will be able to lift your eyes from your text to make contact with your audience. Then you can go back to the text, pick up the first few words of the next paragraph, lift your eyes, and contact the audience.

That is why the text you rehearse should be spaced and paragraphed exactly as you will deliver it. The mind will have "photographed" these paragraph chunks ahead of time; if you disarrange the paragraphing, you will blur the photograph. Don't hesitate to use CAPITAL letters and <u>underlines</u> in your written text to let you know when to emphasize, as well as to help you lift that sentence or word out of the speech for "special handling."

Using underlining, capital letters, and dashes, even circling a word or two, helps you keep the rhythm alive. These marks are crutches to keep you from stumbling.

Such visual cues are the speech aids of professionals. They make the difference between a mediocre speech, laggardly delivered, and a good speech, balanced, keyed, cadenced, lending the dynamism of the spoken word to your written text.

Let me take you through a speech that may be rightly valued as one of the finest examples of American oratory of the last century: the inaugural address of John F. Kennedy, delivered at the East Front of the Capitol, on January 20, 1961.

I have abridged the speech and inserted in the lines the kinds of visual aids you can use. Practice this speech yourself, to see how you would deliver it.

We observe today <u>not</u> a victory of party, but a celebration of freedom—symbolizing an <u>end</u> as well as a <u>beginning</u>—signifying <u>renewal</u>—as well as <u>change</u>.

For I have sworn before <u>you</u> and <u>Almighty God</u> the <u>same</u> solemn oath our forebears prescribed nearly a century and three quarters ago.

The world is <u>very</u> different now.

For man holds in his mortal hands the power to abolish all forms of human poverty—AND all forms of human life.

And yet, the same revolutionary beliefs for which our forebears fought are still at issue around the globe—the belief that the <u>rights of man</u> come <u>NOT</u> from the generosity of the state—but from the hand of <u>God</u>.

Note that I have made each sentence its own paragraph. Underlining marks those words that need to be punctuated with your voice. The dashes represent those oh-so-brief pauses that give a little more lilt and emphasis to the clauses or sentences that follow. The pauses are almost imperceptible, but they are there to give special force to what is being said. Underlining words so that you can emphasize them allows your speech to have some cadence, to avoid monotone. A speech delivered all at the same tone level can become a tad boring to your listener.

If you have "photographed" the speech in your mind, when your eyes fasten on the first phrase—"We observe today <u>not</u> a victory of party"—you will be able to raise your eyes to look at the audience (and the camera) as you say "symbolizing an <u>end</u> as well as a <u>beginning</u>"; the eyes drop ever so briefly to pick up the next phrase—"signifying <u>renewal</u>"—and then are raised again as you speak the last clause, "as well as <u>change</u>."

Carry on with the next paragraph, an easy one to handle without reading more than the first few words.

Continue through the speech, very briefly glance down to pick up the key words in the next sentence, then look up again to speak the rest of the words.

Go on to Kennedy's next paragraph.

> We dare not forget today that we are the heirs of that <u>first</u> revolution.

> Let the word go forth <u>from this time</u>—and <u>from this place</u>—to friends and foes alike—that the torch has passed to a NEW generation of Americans—<u>born</u> in this century—<u>tempered</u> by war—<u>disciplined</u> by a hard and bitter peace—<u>proud</u> of our ancient heritage—and <u>unwilling</u> to witness or permit the slow undoing of those human rights to which this nation has <u>always</u> been committed—and to which we are committed <u>today</u>—at <u>home</u> and around the <u>world</u>.

The key phrases are lifted out, emphasized, and held up for the audience to hear and understand.

The first sentence is the standard-bearer of what is to follow. Thus, when the phrase "let the word go forth <u>from this time</u> and <u>from this place</u>" is spoken, it is opening the door to what is to follow, the eloquent, short, vivid phrases that provide amplification.

When the words are strung together, the mounting drama of the speech is softened, permitted to go a touch lax, but if they are framed by an ever-so-brief pause, there is heft to the words.

Continue now to the paragraph oft quoted in the years that followed, sometimes in criticism of the president's theme (by those who quarreled at a later time about Vietnam and America's role as world policeman) but never to discredit the splendor of the words.

> Let <u>every</u> nation know—whether it wishes us well or <u>ill</u>—that we will pay <u>any</u> price—bear <u>any</u> burden—meet <u>any</u> hardship—support <u>any</u> friend— oppose <u>any</u> foe—to assure the <u>survival</u> and the <u>success</u> of liberty.

There is imposed here a deliberate rhythm that is the mark of a truly great speech. The rise and fall of the clauses, the immediacy of the moment, the heightening of intensity.

Rhythm, like the fluid movements of a great dancer or superb athlete, is essential to the graceful exposition of a line, a thought, or a theme.

Sentences must not collide with one another, thereby breaking up their rhythm. The late Edward Bennett Williams, the most celebrated of Washington lawyers, once mused about how he had learned the prime importance of not bunching his prose in one congealed hunk. "Mrs. Fitzgerald, my English teacher in high school," he recalled, "would rap my knuckles when I indulged in SRT (sentences running together). I used to flunk law students when I taught law at Yale and Georgetown when they could not express themselves correctly. Of course," he grinned, "you can't flunk students today on that count."

In a monograph on music, critic Alan Rich wrote: "The composer satisfied memory by furnishing the listener with memorable materials (usually a melody but just as easily a sonority, a rhythm, or even, conceivably, a certain length of silence) and by bringing back those materials from time to time to let the listeners become oriented and suspect the presence of an orderly process of departure and return. Sometimes the materials are returned verbatim, sometimes they are altered."

This is the measure of the importance of rhythm in speaking. Now, to the denouement of the JFK speech, and its most memorable line:

> And so my fellow Americans—ask <u>not</u> what your country can do for <u>you</u>—ask what <u>you</u> can do for your country.

And so on to the closing lines:

> With a good conscience our only <u>sure</u> reward— with history the <u>final</u> judge of our deeds—<u>let us</u>

> go forth to lead the land we love—asking His
> blessing and His help—but knowing that here on
> earth God's work must be truly our own.

The eye picks up the first phrase, "With a good conscience our only sure reward." Now lift your eyes to challenge your audience with a full gaze as you speak the next
line. Your need to return to the typescript will depend on
how thorough your preparation has been. Remember that
the rhythm of your speaking voice will be affected by the
direction of your gaze. *Never* read. Use your eyes—and
your thorough preparation—to let the text be a guide,
not your sole means of support.

Anyone who chooses to be professional in the delivery of a speech should take one more preparatory step:
Speak what you intend to say into a tape recorder, in
front of a mirror, so that you can practice both eye
contact with the audience and the rhythm and cadence
of your vocal presentation. Time yourself with a stopwatch, if you can, to keep track of the length of your
speech.

The following practice is the best preparatory work
you can do.

1. Read over the text several times; read it out loud.
   Try to get the feel of the words, and connect the
   ideas so that you feel comfortable with what you
   are saying.

2. Stand in front of a mirror. Either hold the text in your hand at about the level of a lectern or place it on a table high enough to resemble a lectern.

3. Begin to read your speech. This time, however, start the rhythm of looking down at the first line, speaking it, and then letting your eye pick up the next several words or the next complete sentence. Now bring your eyes up to face your image in the mirror as you speak the next few words or sentence.

   Eyes back to the text as you speak the next line; then repeat the sequence: Let your eyes "float" ahead to pick up the next sentence, and look up to face your audience.

4. Continue this pattern through the entire speech. Don't worry about stumbling or forgetting. This is practice, and in practice you are aiming to get the feel and the sense of your speech. The time to make errors or to be awkward is in these practice moments.

5. Consider what you have done. Do you think you have managed to confront your audience at least half the time? That is, have you made eye contact as often and for as long as you have been buried in your text?

   Think about this and be honest with yourself. Then begin again and repeat the sequence.

6. Try in the next practice sessions to increase the time of eye contact with the audience and lessen the time of reading. Do it again and again.

You will discover that you can, after a while, increase substantially the percentage of time in which your eyes are on your audience and not on your text. There is no cause for you to feel as if you are walking a tightrope across the Grand Canyon—your text is there before you, a nice soft mattress for you to fall on. But eventually, as your percentage improves, your own sense of confidence (and exhilaration) will ascend dramatically.

7. Once you feel comfortable with the speech and the words become hospitable companions, concentrate on the sound of your voice and the emphasis you give to those phrases you want to point up for your audience in order to persuade them.

8. Consider the overall time of your speech. You may want to edit your text to decrease the total speaking time.

I can pledge you that all this drudgery—and sometimes it may seem precisely that—has a splendid payoff. When you stand before whatever group you address, you will be more confident, more poised than you thought possible, and when you are done, you will probably give your performance a higher rating than you had previously imagined you could. There are few experiences you will savor with more exquisite aftertaste than the successful delivery of a good speech to a responsive audience. Particularly satisfying is the knowledge that because you prepared yourself with rigorous attention to detail, unaided by partners or group effort or grant of favor from any benefactor, you mastered the moment and were, for a brief span of time, triumphant.

It is absolutely essential that you look at your audience. You must not bury your face in your printed text, ignoring the living, breathing people in front of you. Even when you have to drop your gaze to pick up a word or two, suspend contact with the audience for only a few moments.

To do this with ease, you must prepare, practice. There is no known substitute for preparation.

How often—oh, God, how often?—have you sat and listened to a speaker trudge monotonously on, eyes fastened to reading text, voice focused on typescript, clutching each word, and losing all rapport with an audience that by now has stopped looking at their watches and has started to examine the calendar.

My old friend David Brinkley, among the two or three best network news anchormen ever to preside over an evening news show, once amusedly described to me his appearance at a meeting of the Illinois Bankers Association. Brinkley's turn at the rostrum was preceded by a fellow lugging a large briefcase, which he proceeded to place on top of the lectern; he opened it, thrashed through it, pages fluttering, knocked over a water glass, and finally extracted from beneath the pile the speech he was looking for. It was a ten-page document, and the gentleman, provided with neither humor nor eye contact, proceeded to read the entire speech, causing terminal fatigue to run through the audience like a viral contagion. Brinkley sat in horror that was mixed with genuine awe that anyone could continue so without apparent frustration or embarrassment.

In preparing a speech from a written text, you cannot spend too much time burning every word into your memory. Photograph every paragraph in your mind.

The eight-step preparatory exercise outlined on pages 26–28 can be your escape from the written text. When you are no longer a slave to print, the audience will rejoice in your freedom. If you have prepared sufficiently, I warrant you that it is quite possible to drop your eyes seldom and then only to refresh your vision of your "photograph."

Too many high-stationed business executives forage among balance sheets and variable budgets with unerring instinct, but inflict on audiences what *New York Times* columnist William Safire has described as MEGO (My Eyes Glaze Over). The quality of public speaking in the American business community is on a level lower than can be measured by most precision instruments. I have been witness to performances of chairmen and presidents—men who stride their corporate corridors with firm and decisive step but, when on a speaker's rostrum, combine all the lesser traits of Mush Mouth Mulligan with the inspiration of a fellow reciting the latest Lithuanian bond prices.

Alongside corporate captains, place great scientists, labor leaders, and Nobel Prize winners. This country is long on elected officials who address eager audiences ready to be informed and inspired—and soon those present are measuring the distance to the nearest exit. I recall listening to an influential labor leader who commanded the legions of one of the most important unions in the nation. I now understand why his colleagues used to say, "He can empty a hall faster than someone shouting *fire!*"

Making contact with an audience with your eyes is not a guarantee of inspired oratory. But you will have eliminated the largest deterrent to a satisfactory speech. You will have held at least a portion of their interest, because you have not cut the lifeline to their attention.

The late Louis Nizer, the famous courtroom attorney and in his prime one of the finest platform speakers in America (whose book *Thinking on Your Feet* is a classic in the art of speaking) wrote in his autobiography, *Reflections Without Mirrors*:

Professor John Dewey drew large classes at Columbia College because of his eminence, but he suffered the highest absences. He was as dull orally as he was profound in his writings. Professor Albert Einstein did not need the aid of his accent to be incomprehensible. His eyes were buried in his script. His words in monotone emerged haltingly from behind his mustache, losing volume as they were sifted through hair. Audiences rushed to see and hear him, and after they had satisfied their eyes, they closed their ears. Ultimately, they turned to small talk among themselves while the great man droned on. His best oration was at a commencement exercise where he was one of the speakers. He arose and said, "I do not have any particular thoughts to express today, so I wish you all success in your future years." Then he sat down. If only others who had nothing to say would follow his example.

The speaker must see his audience, look into their eyes, observe their facial expressions, and communicate directly to them as participants.

Those of us who remember President John F. Kennedy delivering his inaugural address can readily recall the excitement that brought fire to our veins as the young president spoke. His face, alive and passionate, was lifted toward his audience, drawing us to him, extinguishing our fears, revitalizing our faith. He talked to us, not to his text.

Yet I also remember the first time I heard John Kennedy speak, sometime in 1956. He focused on his text, voiced in an unfamiliar accent (in Texas we found his pronunciation odd), plunging ahead with head bowed over the typescript of his speech; our center of attention was the top of his full head of thickly gardened brown hair, since that was the portion of him most visible to his auditors.

James MacGregor Burns, historian and chronicler of the Kennedy years, once wrote of Senator John Kennedy's maiden speech in the Senate on May 18, 1953:

> Loaded with facts and specific proposals (for New England) the speech sounded very much like an economics lecture at the Harvard Business School. Kennedy spurned rhetoric and oratorical eloquence. He did not bother with any stories, jokes or even illustrative references for "human interest." He simply drove straight along his course.

But Kennedy determined that he would do better. Early on he recognized that he needed another arrow in his quiver: He would apply his talents to becoming a good speaker. His own natural skills were brought to a high polish. He quickly realized that when all else failed, a ready humor would cover mistakes and defuse a hostile audience.

When campaigning for the presidency, he began to develop and practice his art. At a press conference, a reporter dropped a grenade on him. "Do you think a Protestant can be elected president in 1960?" The transcript recorded there was "laughter."

Kennedy smiled warmly and said: "If he's prepared to answer how he stands on the issue of the separation of the Church and State, I see no reason why we should discriminate against him."

The entire press corps broke up in a howl of laughter.

In the span of time between 1956 and his inaugural in 1960, he perfected a style of speaking that was replete with wit and urbanity and, most of all, he acquired the ability to find his way through a prepared text without clinging to it, as a frightened child clutches his mother's skirt.

He learned. So can you.

While style and rhythm are important, the gritty details of the speaking environment matter too. Professional speakers and public officials all know this.

Requisite to any well-delivered speech, beyond the essentials of preparation, is to know where you are speaking, to whom you are speaking, the logistics and layout of the hall, and the atmosphere of the event.

Keep a checklist of items you want to know about in advance.

The Preparation

1. Where is the speech to be delivered? Is it in a large room or a small one? How many people will be in attendance? If it is a small room, can you dispense with a microphone and still be audible to the assembled people? If a microphone is indicated, do you want a stand-up mike at the lectern, or a lavaliere (to be hung around your neck), or a handheld mike with a long cord, or—what I like best—a tiny mike attached to your tie and connected to a tiny switch-box you can attach to your belt out of sight of the audience. This gives you more freedom of movement.

2. Always ask for a lectern of some kind, unless you are going to speak without notes. The lectern is useful in two ways: It can hold your notes or text, and it is a pillar, a life preserver if you don't know what to do with your hands. You can hold on to its sides. You can lean against it. Whatever you feel most comfortable with, whatever eases your nervousness and makes you feel better about speaking, make use of.

3. What kind of audience is this? Is it a homogeneous group—that is, are they all coming to hear you because of a shared interest—or are they from differing groups and backgrounds? For example, you may be speaking to the local Lion's Club. The

audience are all members of the same club, but they all come from disparate backgrounds. On the other hand, if you are speaking to the local chapter of the Cost Accountants Association, your audience has at least one connecting link that binds them together. You need to know who the audience is, and why they have assembled.

Whatever the topic of your speech, always try to insert in the beginning of the speech (or in the middle, where it is least expected) some inside joke or thought particularly pertinent to the people who are listening to you. Whether they are bankers or security analysts or meat-packers, find out something about them, their business, some of their best-known leaders, and add to your text a few lines directly targeted to this particular audience. You are guaranteed an appreciative, embracing response.

4. What is the format? Who will introduce you? Are you the only speaker? If not, who precedes you and who follows you, and what are they speaking about? If the format is a panel discussion, who are your fellow panel members, and how is the panel to operate? Do they want you to make an opening statement, or will the moderator simply begin the discussion? Will there be questions from the audience?

5. What is your subject to be and how much time is allocated to your part of the program? Always try

to give back a few minutes of the allotted time. Nothing so surprises and gratifies arranging committees as to deal with a speaker who is eager to shorten rather than lengthen time allotments.

6. Are you speaking from a platform or is there some other arrangement? Will the audience be seated entirely in front of you or will they surround you, as in a theater in the round? Is there to be a head table, or will you rise and speak at your own table, or are you to sit in the audience until you are called to speak? Do you wait until you have been formally introduced to go to the rostrum, or do you sit in a designated location near the introducer?

7. Will there be a question-and-answer period, and if so, how long will it be? How are the mechanics of recognizing the questioners to be handled? Will they rise in the audience, or are their questions to be written out in advance and handed up to the emcee to read aloud? Who will call a halt to the questions, and in what manner? (You should never end the question period yourself, but always arrange in advance for the emcee to shut off the audience response.)

8. Are you speaking at a luncheon or dinner, or at a business meeting of some kind? If no formal meal

is involved, will refreshments be served before, or during, the meeting? At what time will you go on?

If you are an after-dinner speaker keep in mind several points: People who have been sitting for over an hour, pouring down drinks, eating heartily, talking incessantly to their dinner companions, are not usually eager to be regaled with a long program. After-dinner speaking is the toughest obstacle course to traverse successfully. This is the time for a brief speech, never longer than fifteen minutes. The shorter the speech, the more merciful you will appear to your audience and the more enthusiastically they will applaud your understanding of their plight. They are hostages praying for release.

For an after-dinner speech, always find out the order of the program. If you have a choice, be the first to speak after the meal. Dinner guests will be more attentive and a bit more appreciative of the first speaker. Their enthusiasm and their patience decrease with each speaker who follows.

If you are to be an after-luncheon speaker, always remember that 2 P.M. is the favorite quitting time. If you can't finish by 2 P.M., finish anyway, or you will be bedeviled by the shuffling of chairs and the hunched-over exit of a good many of your audience. While you may know that what you are saying is well worth listening to, the clock is inexorable and deaf to your voice.

9. Finally, be prepared in advance to respond to a lavish introduction. First, you should keep your eyes on the person introducing you, so that if the introduction is particularly flowery, you can avoid embarrassment by avoiding the eyes of the audience. Second, you should smile deprecatingly when the introducer carries on a little too fulsomely about your achievements and your splendid charm. Let the audience know that you know the speaker is laying it on a bit thick.

Another advantage accrues from keeping your gaze on the person introducing you. Your own first eye contact with the audience becomes a little more dramatic when you rise to speak—you are now "seeing" them for the first time, and you are in command of their full attention.

In summary, attention to every detail is the mark of a professional, of someone who cares very much about doing the best job possible. Only by knowing all there is to know about your subject, your audience, the environment of the meeting, the type and timing of the program, and your own well-thought-out plan of response, will you be sufficiently armed to take up the challenge and be successful. You will never fall through a crack in the floor if you have mapped the territory in advance.

CHAPTER THREE

The Length

*How Long You Should Speak, and
Why You Should Not Speak Long*

The best way to begin this chapter is to quote a gentleman who was the first—other than the prophets of the Bible—to declare the value of a compact speech. Saint Ambrose, Bishop of Milan in the fourth century, wrote, "Let us have a reason for beginning and let our end be within due limits. For a speech that is wearisome only stirs up anger."

To the reasons for Saint Ambrose's canonization please add his full appreciation of the value of brevity and substance.

It is my conviction, based on years of being put upon by all manner of public speakers, that twenty minutes is the absolute maximum that anyone should allow for a speech. It is a known fact that Fidel Castro inflicts on his audiences speeches of an hour, even two or three hours. Indeed, it is recorded that on his ascendancy to the post of chairman of the Communist Party in the People's Republic of China (a position formerly occupied by Mao Zedong), Hua Guofeng spoke to the faithful for over three and a half hours. Without stopping. It is also a known fact that those who listen to such speeches have meager alternatives.

The late Vice President Hubert Humphrey, one of the greatest platform speakers I ever heard, was notorious for going beyond what may be judged the absolute limit. On occasions I counted as many as eight "climax" opportunities during a campaign speech, moments when if he had bowed and said thank you, he would have concluded in a blaze of glory. But each time, the irrepressible vice president continued on, sweeping to a new curve of oratory while the audience, ready to applaud, sat back again and waited. And waited.

But Humphrey was an anomaly, an original. He seldom spoke from a written text, preferring to extemporize, an ability born of countless hours on the stump, where he honed and perfected his special style. Humphrey was one of the few speakers I have known who could invest his speech with humor—self-deprecating, belly-splitting humor—without the aid of professional funnymen. Like most originals, he broke every rule in the book and got away with it, because he possessed inexhaustible resources of eloquence, and made skillful and awe-inspiring use of what Francis Bacon once described as "the choiceness of the phrase, the round and clean composition of the sentence, and the sweet falling of the clauses."

The Length

Before mounting the speaker's rostrum, make sure you have practiced your written speech not only for form, memory, and familiarity, but also for time. A rule of thumb is that one 8½ by 11 typed page, double-spaced, will hold about two minutes' worth of spoken material. Therefore, you can usually judge that eight pages of script will run about sixteen minutes. But practice and practice again. If you find your speech rhythms run more than two minutes per page, edit, cut, reduce. Keep the speech under twenty minutes—fifteen is more desirable, and ten minutes is great. Remember this maxim: *It is difficult to make a bad speech out of a short speech*.

Even the most talented speakers fall prey to the "endless" speech. I recall I was once invited to sit on the dais at a mammoth gathering sponsored by the prestigious City Club of New York. The featured speaker was Daniel Patrick Moynihan, then the U.S. Ambassador to the United Nations, later an influential senator from New York, now retired.

Pat Moynihan is a rarity, a gifted intellectual and orator brimming over with a wild Irish wit, a prodigal elfin charm that mixes with his own unique recipe of literate bite and splendor. This evening, however, Moynihan delivered an erudite civics lecture, packed with statistics ill-suited to an audience heavily weighted with business proconsuls who had a low threshold of interest in the socioeconomics of urban sprawl—a speech altogether more fitting for an auditorium full of Harvard doctoral candidates. He spoke for over forty minutes, and during

the last twenty-five there was restlessness among the na-
tives. When he finally finished, the sighs of relief could
have inflated the Graf zeppelin. Moynihan came with a
deserved reputation as a wit and a charmer and left with
the—also deserved—label of "professor."

Some months later I heard Pat Moynihan on a live TV
show in New York. He was absolutely brilliant. He spoke
concisely, each word splendidly apt, and tossed off witty
sentences with the grace of a verbal Baryshnikov. It was
his brevity that gave force to what he said.

How to explain the City Club speech? Even Ted Williams and Joe DiMaggio used to strike out occasionally.

Some years ago, I was one of those on a glittering dais
at the annual meeting of the Friars Club (a show-
business–oriented organization), honoring Henry Kissinger. In the Grand Ballroom of the Waldorf-Astoria in
New York, the audience was composed of the well-
known, the well-heeled, and the short-patienced. Kirk
Douglas was master of ceremonies and I took the precau-
tionary measure of consulting with him ahead of time.
How many speakers, Kirk? Nine? Ye gods, then when do
I go on? Number six? Ouch, that I don't like. Who is first
on the program? Barbara Walters? Okay, then, let me go
on second. Can you do that? That's fine. My reason: The
longer the list of speakers, the less patient the audience
becomes as the evening winds on. I always like to be no
later than the middle of the speaking lineup. After a full
meal, and a certain drinking routine, as the hour gets late,
audience decay sets in.

On the dais was an array of the famous: Gregory Peck, William Buckley, the ambassadors of Egypt and Israel, Frank Sinatra, Mike Wallace, movie/televisoin mogul Barry Diller, the heads of the three major TV networks, the mayor of New York, and assorted other folks well known to newspaper readers and television viewers. There was also a comedian-singer waiting in the wings to entertain.

The audience awaiting this lineup of movie stars, television commentators, and the fabled in public affairs and journalism would be eager to hear them out—until the mesmerizing enchantment wore off and ennui began to infect the hall.

Barbara Walters rose and in two and a half minutes issued a most congenial and witty presentation.

I got to my feet, tongue readied for a one-minute thirty-second essay. Barbara had set a standard for brevity that I vowed to uphold, even to surpass.

My offering:

> *Only in America—only in America!*
> *Born in middle Europe, the young lad immigrates to America and learns a second language, which even now gives off in every sentence he speaks the aroma of his origins.*
>
> *The boy grown to manhood becomes a professor at one of the most prestigious universities in the United States. He writes books with persuasive designs to bring harmony to a disordered*

world. Washington's foreign-policy makers coun-
sel with him, and then one day his political party,
after eight years in exile, returns to power, and
with the new president he comes to Washington,
this time garmented in the powerful robes of Na-
tional Security Adviser to the president of the
United States. This foreign-born immigrant is now
the chief architect of foreign policy. I salute the
man who has lived this life: Zbigniew Brzezinski!

A frail piece of humor, dear Henry. For I bear
you great affection and respect.

For no man knows better how to be luminous,
or how to be obscure.

This is you, Henry, and if Lord Macaulay had
not written those words about William Pitt the
Younger, I like to believe that I would have writ-
ten them about you.

I confess to limitations, one of which is plainly the
absence of any talent for stand-up comedy. Whenever I
try to be humorous, it is only for a sentence or two, never
more than a paragraph. Sustaining a comedic theme may
seem easy. It is not.

Therefore, I got on and got off as quickly as I could.
I am pleased to note I garnered one laugh, and one
chuckle abandoned before it got to the belly-churning
stage. For me, not a bad catch.

As I could have predicted, the example of brevity set

by Barbara and me was not long emulated. Two more speakers were admirably brief, and then the clock turned into a calendar. One speaker, who shall remain nameless, to my horror plucked from his inside pocket what looked to be a sheaf of documents suitable for a legal deposition. He placed them on the rostrum, adjusted his glasses, and galloped off into a discourse about the fate of the nation that had only sporadic relevance to the guest of honor. He was followed by two others who between them consumed twenty-five more minutes, and one could have charted on a graph the descending, soon to be avalanching, level of interest on the part of the audience, culminating in a nodding of heads and blinking of heavy lids.

But lessons of brevity are learned by bitter experience. Just before he abandoned television, I was on another Friars Club dais, this time honoring Johnny Carson. As it would be again, the dais was laden with the best-known people in the land. Then, too, there were eight or nine speakers and the inevitable entertainer. The night wore on. When the entertainer finally bounded onto the stage to do his bit, I could see Johnny Carson looking at his watch. When the singular performer of this generation checks his watch, you know there is a heavy sea ahead.

When Carson at last got to his feet, smiling wanly, the crowd stirred in reawakened interest. The nonpareil Carson jauntily offered a few funny lines, then a few serious lines, thanked the Friars and the audience for their honor, and promptly sat down. Total time on the air: two minutes. The old pro had sniffed the air and resolved to flush out just one covey of laughs and call it a night.

Interminable programs are an affliction that have no known cure.

In Los Angeles, Don Rickles was the principal speaker at a meeting of a group of medical men and women. The selection of Don Rickles as the main attraction does bespeak a certain courage—not to say foolhardiness—among the medical profession. There was a lengthy program before Mr. Rickles was supposed to be introduced. The program came down with lingering filibusteritis. It went on and on, and many doctors in the audience with early morning appointments quietly shuffled out of the hall.

Some minutes past midnight when Rickles was called on to do his number, he rose, glared at the now diminished but hardy crowd, leaned into the microphone, and speared the program's architect with: "Let's face it, folks. This evening just fell on its ass," and hustled off the stage.

The shorter the speech, the better your chances of success. There is an enduring maxim everyone ought to memorize: "Always leave at the height of a party," meaning wherever you are, stop talking when your listeners expect, and want, you to keep going.

Let me summarize about length:

The Length

1. If you are speaking after dinner at a large gathering
    of several hundred people who have already en-
    dured a long cocktail hour and exhausted all their
    conversational charm on the person next to them,
    and if there are no more than one or two other
    speakers, keep your speech under six or seven
    minutes. If you are the only speaker on the program,
    with perhaps some minor and brief presentations,
    you can extend to the fifteen- to twenty-minute
    boundary, but fifteen is better. After that you are
    swimming in a riptide.

2. If you are one of several after-dinner speakers, and
    indeed may also share the platform with some en-
    tertainment, your remarks should be under five
    minutes in length. The shorter the better. There are
    few more deadly actions to take than to drone on
    for ten minutes or more when you are preceded and
    followed by others who may follow your bad ex-
    ample, to the visible dismay of the audience.

3. If you are speaking to a college class, or are the only
    speaker at a seminar or a forum convened for the
    sole purpose of hearing you, then you may and
    should extend your remarks to thirty minutes.
    When the chairman of such an event allots you
    forty-five minutes to an hour, smile politely and re-
    solve to give him back a portion of that time. You

will win the hearts of your audience and you may devote whatever time is left to questions and answers.

4. If you are an after-luncheon speaker, there is usually a set time for adjournment. Keep your eye on your watch, and when you are introduced you will know precisely how much time is left. Even if your chairman is a lenient, hospitable fellow who says you may go beyond the quitting time, don't. If you continue beyond the cutoff hour you will be greeted by the thump of departing feet. Get off on time.

5. If you are speaking at a business, professional, or technical convention, always remember that you are only one of a legion of folks who will harangue the gathering. Keep what you are going to say compact and to the point. If you appear at a morning session after a long night of socializing by most of the convention participants, it is a certifiable fact that an interminable lecture will be as welcome as wild elephants mating in the living room. Measure the length of your talk by its nature: In a technical seminar where the audience has come to learn specifically what you have come to teach, you may extend your time with small fear of audience boredom. But if your subject is not concretely defined and detailed, be wary, and be brief. At such conventions question-and-answer periods fill in any unwelcome gaps.

CHAPTER FOUR

The Delivery

*How to Speak with Notes
and without Them*

The ultimate ambition of a good speaker is to create rapport with the audience. What a decisive piece of language is that French word, *rapport. Rapport* is an embrace, an affectionate warmth, a mutual reaching out, a harmonious friendliness that is the warranty of affinity and concord among people.

The prime element in constructing rapport is eye contact with those who are listening to you. Therefore, the less you refer to a written text, the more you make that indispensable eye contact, the essential first source of rapport with your audience.

Moreover, the audience senses that a written text could have been composed by someone other than the speaker (in most cases it is). They tend to offer a more hospitable reception to what they perceive to be the speaker's own thoughts than to the ideas of an unknown scribe.

Believability is the largest asset a speaker can project. Your own words, words that flow from your heart and brain, fall on more receptive ears. If you are believable, you can stumble, fumble (not too much, now, just a bit), and still finish with the feeling that your audience is nodding in agreement. Believability is more easily attained when you appear to be thinking for yourself rather than mouthing words like a ventriloquist's dummy. That is why speaking from notes—or without them—is better than reading from a prepared text.

In his abridged version of Plato's works, Henry L. Drake wrote of Plato: "He spoke without notes and recommended that few notes be taken because he thought that written words tend to escape the mind. It was his belief that repetition and meditation, rather than many notes, are the proper aids to memory."

There is little question that speaking without notes is the most powerful form of communication. You have full command of the audience. There is nothing to interfere with what you are saying. You are looking at the audience and they at you with no paper barriers. It is the most suitable medium for persuasion. But it is also the riskiest.

Plato was right about repetition and meditation being the proper aids to sealing a speech in one's mind. Prerequisite to speaking without notes is an exacting regimen, going over what you are going to say, again and again and again. I would also recommend writing out the speech in full in advance.

The Delivery

Don't trust to inspiration. Unless you are a consummate professional, trained and skilled by countless hours of speaking before numberless groups, inspiration will poop out on you when you need it most. I accept more speaking engagements than I should simply to keep my speaking skills honed. The more one speaks before audiences, the more professionally confident one becomes. And the obverse is also true: The less one speaks, the rustier one becomes.

It would seem logical that elected public officials, some of whom have spent the greater part of their adult life in the electoral cockpit, would be more comfortable in speaking on TV or before crowds. Yet, if you watch the Congress in speaking action on C-Span, you may be struck by the inability of too many members to rise for one, two, three minutes without a written text in front of them. Why this reliance on a text by those who ought to be the most professional in rising to persuade an audience? Usually the member rises to speak on a subject he or she probably knows pretty well, else why confront it? I suspect the reliance on a written text for the minute or so the member is speaking is mainly because of expediency. It's just easier to rely on a written text. You don't have to work as hard. It is, alas, the endless battle between a busy schedule and a reluctance to spend the required energy and time versus doing it right. Usually schedule, time, and energy win. Yet, to my bewilderment, a good many men and women do succeed in politics without ever becoming what I would describe as "an adequate public speaker."

But there are others who excel. The young senator from North Carolina, John Edwards (elected in 1998), has mastered with exquisite skill the no-notes speech. Doubtless this ascendancy as an engaging speaker emerges from Senator Edwards's years of mesmerizing juries in his many years as a courtroom lawyer, one of the nation's most successful plaintiff's attorneys. He is a formidable machine in action. I don't know whether Senator Edwards writes out his speeches in advance. Nonetheless, he obviously possesses a prodigious memory and an improvisatory technique that allows him literally to compose the greater part of what he is saying at the moment he says it, or at least he gives an audience that impression. I do not recommend this routine to anyone who is not thoroughly confident and considerably talented, which is an accurate description of Senator Edwards.

Before he retired from the Senate a few years ago, none matched Senator Dale Bumpers, of Arkansas, as a freewheeling orator, who roamed the Senate chamber with nary a note in his hand as he regaled his colleagues. Another recently retired senator, Alan Simpson of Wyoming, had no peer in using homespun humor extracted from cowboy on-the-range lore. Again without written notes or text.

Another complete professional on a rostrum, without notes, is Robert Strauss, former ambassador to Russia.

Indeed, Strauss is visibly less effective when he works from a written text than when he is devoid of any notes. Strauss's principal weapon is wit, sometimes sharp-edged, Texas-bred humor, casually offered, and usually saucy, skittering along the borderline between what is just right and what is embarrassingly wrong. It is a testament to Strauss's skill on the stump that he invariably walks the edge of the precipice, but never falls off.

In the last 125 years (so my research informs me) every president has delivered his Inaugural Address with a written text. Except one. Who was he? I doubt if anyone on a quiz show would ever get the correct answer. The answer is Grover Cleveland, the twenty-second (and twenty-fourth) president. In his biography of Cleveland, author H. Paul Jeffers described the scene on March 4, 1885, as follows:

> Once the oath was taken, the twenty-second President of the United States stepped to the podium to deliver his inaugural address, and to secure a place in the history of such speeches by making it without a manuscript. As astonished as every one of the onlookers, but perhaps not aware of the deserved reputation of "Big Steve" Cleveland (the president's first name was Stephen, but he chose to be called Grover) as a winning card player, Senator John J. Ingalls murmured, "God, what a magnificent gambler!"

The onlookers that day stirred with amazement, said Mr. Jeffers, at "the composure of a man . . . who in less than three years rose from an obscure lawyer in a small city and yet was able to stand below the Capitol dome and speak to them of his goals without a note before him, flawlessly."

Cleveland's high-wire performance is all the more astounding since the printed text of what he said that day ran to more than five pages!

It is a matter of record that of all the presidents after Cleveland, none chose to gamble. They all were comforted as they spoke by the full text of what they wanted to say in front of them.

What President Cleveland did, however, was no feat of legerdemain. It was the result of some hard work in advance, though his contemporaries claimed he had a prodigious memory. Of a speech he had written out in advance, he could speak close to an hour without "changing a word or phrase." Whether that is true or not, his Inaugural Address that March day in 1885 is a solid piece of confirmable history. It made me lift Grover Cleveland higher in my rankings of presidents.

A few years ago I was the principal speaker at the Federal Communications Bar Association, in Washington, D.C. After being introduced, I approached the rostrum, lifted the microphone out of its niche, and then stood in front of the lectern so there was no barrier in front of me. I had an unobstructed view of the audience, and vice versa. In my hands I had no text, no notes. The audience saw this instantly.

For a specific purpose, I reproduce here the entire speech. I confess I was pleased when William Safire, the celebrated *New York Times* columnist, included this speech in his best-selling volume *Lend Me Your Ears: Great Speeches in History*. Here is the speech as it appeared in Safire's volume (I have made minor deletions):

> *I would like to talk tonight about what I have learned since I arrived in the Federal City aboard Air Force One on November 22, 1963 . . .*
>
> *I learned that in the White House there is one enduring standard by which every assistant to the president, every presidential adviser, every presidential consultant must inevitably be measured. Not whether you went to Harvard or Yale, or whether you scored 1600 on your SATs, or whether you are endlessly charming and charismatically enabled or whether you made millions in what we sardonically call "the private sector." These are all attractive credentials that one may wear modestly or otherwise. But when the decision crunch is on in the Oval Office they are all merely tracings on dry leaves in the wind. What does count, the ultimate and only gauge, is whether you have "good judgment."*
>
> *I learned that no presidential decision is ever*

made where the president had all the information he needed to make the decision. There are never enough facts. Very quickly, the decision corridor grows dark, the mapping indistinct, the exit inaccessible. What is not useful are precedents or learned disquisitions by op-ed page pundits, some of whom would be better suited to raising pigeons. Finally, the decision is made on judgment alone. Sometimes the judgment is good. Sometimes it is not.

It is well to remember, as Oscar Wilde once said, that from time to time nothing that is worth knowing can be taught. Judgment is something that springs from some little elf who lives somewhere between your belly and your brain, and who from time to time, tugs at your nerve edges, and says, "No, not that way, the other way." This mysterious inhabitant is called instinct, intuition, judgment. It is the one ingredient on which the rest of the human condition depends for guidance.

I learned that the one political component above all else which can insure electoral victory or crushing defeat is timing. A whack to your political solar plexus six to eight months before an election is survivable. Two weeks before the election, and you're dead. In politics, twenty hours is a millennium.

The Delivery

I learned that economic forecasts beyond about two weeks have the same odds of accuracy as guessing the winning numbers in the lottery. Economic forecasts are usually unwarranted assumptions leaping to a preconceived conclusion. Just remember, whenever an economist can't remember his phone number, he will give you an estimate.

I learned that when there is no unamiable issue like war or prospect of war or recession or economic disaster, most people vote for a president viscerally not intellectually. Most people choose a president romantically, a choice made in unfathomable ways, which is how romance is formed. Which is why voters chose John Kennedy and Ronald Reagan.

I learned never to humiliate an antagonist and never desert a friend. In a political struggle, never get personal else the dagger digs too deep. Your enemy today may need to be your ally tomorrow.

I learned that a political poll is Janus in disguise. The life of a poll is about ten nanoseconds. It is already in decay when it is published. A political poll, like the picture of Dorian Gray, is the face of entropy. The veteran professionals know that. The old pols use polls to raise money. When polls are up, go for the fat wallets. But the politician who persistently lifts his wet finger to test the political polls before he acts, usually leaves office with a wet finger.

But the greatest lesson I have learned, the most important of my education, is really the essential imperative of this century. It is called leadership. We brandish the word. We admire its light. But we seldom define it. Outside Caen in the Normandy countryside of France is a little cemetery. Atop one of the graves is a cross on which is etched these words: "Leadership is wisdom and courage and a great carelessness of self." Which means, of course, that leaders must from time to time put to hazard their own political future in order to do what is right in the long term interests of those they have by solemn oath sworn to serve. Easy to say. Tough to do.

I remember when I first bore personal witness to its doing. It was in December 1963. Lyndon Johnson had been president but a few short weeks. At that time I was actually living on the third floor of the White House until my family arrived. The president said to me on a Sunday morning, "Call Dick Russell and ask him if he would come by for coffee with you and me."

Senator Richard Brevard Russell of Georgia was the single most influential and honored figure in the Senate. His prestige towered over all others in those years before the dialogue turned sour and mean. His one defect was that he was the leader of the segregation forces in the Senate. When in 1952, the Senate Democratic leader's post fell open, the other senators turned immediately to Russell, imploring him to take the job. "No," said Russell, "let's make Lyndon Johnson our leader, he'll do just fine." So at the age of forty-four, just four years into his first Senate term, LBJ became the youngest ever Democratic Senate leader and in a short time the greatest parliamentary commander in that chamber's history.

When Russell arrived, the president greeted him warmly with a strong embrace, the six-foot-four LBJ and the smaller, compact Russell, with his gleaming bald head and penetrating eyes. The president steered him to the couch overlooking the Rose Garden, in the West Hall on the second floor of the Mansion. I sat next to Russell. The president was in his wing chair, his knees almost touching Russell's, so close did they sit.

The president drew even closer, and said in an even voice, "Dick, I love you and I owe you. If it had not been for you I would not have been leader, or vice president or now president. So I owe you. But I wanted to tell you, face to face, please don't get in my way on this Civil Rights Bill, which has been locked up in the Senate too damn long. I intend to pass this bill, Dick. I will not cavil. I will not hesitate. And if you get in my way, I'll run you down."

Russell sat mute for a moment, impassive, his face a mask. Then he spoke, in the rolling accents of his native Georgia countryside. "Well, Mr. President, you may just do that. But I pledge you that if you do, it will not only cost you the election, it will cost you the South forever."

President Johnson in all the later years in which I knew him so intimately never made me prouder than he did that Sunday morning a long, long time ago. He touched Russell lightly on the shoulder, an affectionate gesture of one loving friend to another. He spoke softly, almost tenderly: "Dick, my old friend, if that's the price I have to pay, then I will gladly pay it."

Of all the lessons I have learned in my political life, that real life instruction in leadership was the most elemental, and the most valuable. It illuminated in a blinding blaze the highest point to which the political spirit can soar. I have never forgotten it. I never will.

Later a good many of those in the audience queried me on "how did you do that, no notes, no text," suggesting I pulled off something magical. So what was the secret of the trick? It was no trick, no magic. Anyone could have done it. I truly mean that. My speech was simply the final summary of a good deal of hard work. So when I say "anyone can do it" that admonition must be matched to "if you are willing to do the labor beforehand."

This is the routine I follow:

1. I break the speech into separate paragraphs, to make the task of memory easier. Paragraphing is particularly important in preparing a speech for memorization: Each paragraph should be short and should keep to one theme. The first sentence of each paragraph is a key line that opens the door to the rest of what I will say and I have these key lines absolutely fixed in my mind. Then, even if I cannot remember all the words verbatim, I am still able to improvise from the theme of that opening sentence.

2. I begin by saying aloud, over and over again, the first two paragraphs. I do not worry if I don't say the speech exactly as it was written. But I strive to get the essence of the paragraphs settled firmly in my mind.

3. After I have sufficiently committed the first two paragraphs to memory, I turn my attention to the next two paragraphs. Again the same routine: the speaking aloud of these two prose groupings until they are etched into my mind.

4. Then, for the first time, I put the first four para-
    graphs together and speak them again and again.

5. On to the next two paragraphs. I am by now into
    a disciplined groove of preparation. Within a short
    time I am able to speak with some confidence the
    first six paragraphs of the speech.

A strange thing happens as you go about this learning
assignment. As you gain confidence in your ability to remember, the speed with which the work progresses picks
up considerably. You begin to feel you are making
measurable progress. The effort to memorize is less
drudging, and surely less daunting. Your exhilaration
level rises rapidly.

6. I keep with this routine, moving through the other
    paragraphs, two at a time, then going back and
    picking up the previous paragraphs, repeating them
    over and over again. Once I have finally put to-
    gether the entire speech, I spend a good deal of time
    repeating it to myself. In my car instead of listening
    to the radio or dispatching my mind to some distant
    problem, I say the speech over and over again. In
    the shower and as I shave, I repeat it. I usually keep
    a copy with me (not in the shower—the ink tends
    to run), so that if for some blighted moment my
    memory fails me, I can quickly glance at the written
    text to see what I have momentarily omitted.

7. The day before I am scheduled to speak, I spend an hour or so with my stopwatch and my tape recorder, going over the speech for intonation and for timing. I make certain I will speak no longer than twenty minutes, less if I can.

On the appointed evening, when I rise to begin my speech, I am totally and completely prepared. The hard work is behind me. The actual delivery of the speech becomes great fun for me, solely because I had prepared. Was I gloriously free of some stage fright? No, I wasn't. But, as I said earlier, stage fright is good for you. It unlooses the adrenaline that alerts your brain to be at battle stations. Yes, there always lies in the shadows a fear that you will forget something important, that you will freeze up, and so on. But keep in mind that even if you leave out something, the audience won't know it! But I assure you if you have done the preparatory labor, while you will not mount the speaker's rostrum nerveless and calm, you will have, as Mark Twain once wrote, "the serene confidence of a Christian with four aces up his sleeve." Your "four aces" are your preparatory work.

It was said of Alfred Hitchcock that he assiduously blocked out each scene of his movie in laborious, relentless detail in advance. When production began he knew down to the last jot what he wanted from every scene, what he required from each actor, where the camera was to be placed, etc. The actual filming was a piece of cake. The indispensable work had already been done. Hitchcock could literally compose the filming with few takes, so thoroughly had he absorbed, in rigorous detail, what he wanted in the scene. His intimate friends used to say Hitchcock became a bit bored by the real filming. The fun part in his elaborate storyboards had already been completed. So, just remember in taking on an assignment like this, you must be committed to a regimen of continuous preparation. There is no alternative. Nor should there be. What fun would you have, what rousing spirit of achievement would you feel, if anybody could do it without any work in advance?

One final point. I personally believe that about 800 words is pretty much the outer limit for such memorization (that's about four double-spaced typewritten pages). Anything longer requires more exhaustive preparation than most people are prepared to undertake.

I also believe that a 300- or 400-word presentation (about three to four minutes in time) ought never to be spoken from a prepared text. This length is about two double-spaced typewritten pages, or slightly less. If you are not capable (or, however mistakenly, think you are not capable) of committing to memory a talk of 300 to 400 words, then furnish yourself with some notes using key words and phrases from the final draft of your rehearsed speech.

All this is easy enough to do, if you are willing to work. The quality of your speech will diminish in exact proportion to the time you did not give to this special task of preparation.

Obviously, one doesn't deliver speeches that require such intensive preparation every day. Such a schedule would exhaust anybody. I only make such speeches two or three times a year. Moreover, I do not give the speech in precisely the form in which I wrote it. Few speakers do. I used different phrasing and digressed slightly several times. But I persisted in holding on to the main thought—and my confidence. The prime element in such a speech is knowing the material so well that minor excursions outside the original written text don't unhinge you.

When delivering a speech without notes, don't try to swallow the speech whole—it will give you psychic indigestion. Rather, take the speech one paragraph at a time. Learn the first paragraph, go over it until you have it cold, then take on the second paragraph. Seal it in your memory, and then recap and repeat the first two paragraphs together. When you have those two indelibly in your mind, confront the third paragraph, and so on. Always repeat what you have memorized before you go on to a new paragraph. This is much the same advice that coaches and directors give to actors. Learn your lines piecemeal, enlarging what you have learned each time, so that eventually you will have captured in your memory cells what you need to say.

There are any number of techniques that first-rate speakers use. The late Louis Nizer, one of the greatest of all twentieth-century courtroom lawyers, as well as a best-selling author, was possessed of a speaking armory that was lawyerly, intellectual in its reach and poise, but always invested with enough humor to enliven the audience's grasp. Nizer would seize a subject (what the world will be like in the year 2000, or the age-old quarrel between Israel and Arab nations, or the elusive definition of due process) and totally possess it. His speeches had a beginning, a middle, and an end. He was a master of epigram, the whipcracking phrase to illustrate a point ("When you point one accusing finger at someone, three of your own fingers point back to you"). He spoke in parables, always using a fable or aphorism or engaging phrase to illustrate the point he was making.

Just before he became president, General Eisenhower disclosed some ideas about speaking in public, particularly in reference to memorizing speeches. The general said that Winston Churchill gave him "unshirted hell" for speaking from memory and not following the text of prepared remarks.

Even so, said the general, he did better without a text. "I'm through with prepared speeches, except in those cases where I have to have precise timing, such as radio and television." He said he would do things his own way, with reminder notes of the points he chose to make.

Eisenhower recounted how on one occasion in London, he had a 125-word message to deliver, so he memorized it and delivered it without a hitch. Churchill later reprimanded him severely. Said Churchill: "Never trust your memory in anything like that with people following every word you say to see if you repeated exactly what was written."

Churchill went on to advise Eisenhower to wear spectacles, "big round spectacles you can take off and shake in their face. And if you have notes don't try to hide them. Shake them in their faces, too."

The foxy Sir Winston, arguably the finest orator of his generation, didn't disclose to General Eisenhower that he always wrote out what he wanted to say, then transferred the written text to notes that he scrawled in his own hand or had typed after he had polished them to his satisfaction. This was his unvarying method of preparation, whether for a speech to be delivered in the Commons, an address to a large assembly, or a talk at a political gathering. No matter the locale or the occasion, Churchill laboriously composed his remarks and from the written text constructed his notes, which, as he advised Eisenhower, he brandished without shame to whatever audience he was addressing.

It may be that the one time Churchill did not follow his usual routine was when he returned as prime minister to speak to the students of Harrow, his boyhood school. When the prime minister was introduced, he rose to his feet, one hand tugging at his coat lapel, the other behind his back, and spoke the following words:

"Never give in. Never give in. Never give in, never,

never, never—in nothing great or small, large or petty—
never give in, except to conviction, honor, and good
sense." Whereupon the great man looked solemnly at his
awestruck young audience, and sat down.

The fact is that though Churchill scolded General Eisenhower for his memory work on short speeches, the
prime minister labored diligently and exhaustively over
his important speeches. He did in fact memorize whole
reams of prose and rarely consulted his notes. Unless, of
course, the speech was long, loaded with facts that would
be scrutinized later by those who had heard him, or set
forth a policy declaration whose clarity he did not wish
to cloud with any kind of imprecision, no matter how
eloquently dispatched. The old warrior-author-politician
did his homework, every time.

Speaking from notes, particularly on a rostrum that
is—at least to you—an important one, takes more than
a modest amount of courage. You are, as it were, without
the safety net of a full written text. But with notes you
are not entirely alone. It is a speaker's art form that is,
thankfully, easy to learn.

1. You must understand that preparation for such a
   speech is even more necessary than when you have
   a written text.
2. Don't let it worry you that you will probably never
   deliver a speech from notes the same way you have
   practiced it.

3. You have to become intimately companionable with the words you will speak.
4. Essential to a successful notes-only speech is a firm grasp of the subject on which you are speaking.

If you are planning to speak with notes only to a convention of, say, investment bankers, and you are not an investment banker, have only a superficial knowledge of the subject, and know that once you dip beneath the surface of the subject you will be gasping for air, forget it. Go with a written text. But if you are in the investment banking business, it is quite possible that you do know more than a little about your subject and can manage without a written text. Knowledge of the subject is the soundest armor one can wear.

The primary step is to set down on paper what you want to say. It is always useful to write the speech in full, so that you have before you all you intend to impart to the audience.

Then exercise as before: Read it over, again and again, until you have imprinted in your mind the core essentials of the speech.

Next, break the speech down into subject headings.

Put down in your notes any statistics you will need. If the numbers you will cite must be absolutely accurate, you ought to arm yourself in your notes. Any imprecision is likely to be remarked by your audience.

Keep in mind that speaking from notes requires your knowing your subject so well you can extemporize. Total command of your subject allows you to wander, as it were, because you can always find your way back to the central path from which you have strayed. To repeat the warning: Never try to speak merely from notes unless you know your subject cold.

Always try to commit to memory the last several sentences. The conclusion of a speech is one of its most important elements, often cementing all that you have said or, what is more usual, providing a graceful exit line that will summarize and make memorable what you have hoped to communicate. Memorize that last paragraph.

In May 2000, I was the commencement speaker at the graduation exercises of the University of Oklahoma in Norman. The president of the University is the former governor of and senator from Oklahoma, David Boren. Senator Boren is, himself, one of the finest speakers ever to grace the Senate chamber. Fluid in his delivery, with a masterly sense of the dramatic, Boren commands the total attention of audiences. There is no larger laurel to be sought by a speaker.

In this commencement speech, I drew on the same design I had used in my Federal Communications Bar Association speech, that is, I emulated much the same architecture, the repetition of phrases (note the use of the phrase "It is a gift") for dramatic narrative. I did change the interior design. I delivered this commencement speech without a text, but with notes.

What follows now is the full speech, which was written in advance and from which I drew my notes. I titled the speech: "The Gift of Freedom: Some Thoughts about War, Youth, Politics, and the Mystical Embrace of the U.S. Constitution." Long title, but with enough enticing subjects listed to draw the attention of a prospective audience.

This is the speech:

> Let me begin by quoting that tireless observer of the human scene, Art Buchwald, who told another commencement audience, "We're leaving you a perfect world. Don't screw it up!"
>
> I have been very fortunate. I have been able to spend my entire working career in two of life's classic fascinations, politics and movies. In both worlds I have known the great, the near-great, and those who thought they were great. Guess which category is the most numerous?
>
> I have lived long enough to learn a few things. I am still learning.
>
> I have learned that no one is indispensable, that the light in the White House may flicker, but

the light in the White House never, never goes out. I was in the motorcade in Dallas, six cars back of President John F. Kennedy on November 22, 1963. I was a personal witness to a senseless act of mindless malice, the murder of a young president, slain in the streets of Dallas. I was ordered aboard Air Force One by the new president, to become his first newly hired special assistant. I was in that historic photograph which depicts Lyndon Baines Johnson, thirty-sixth in the line of presidents, taking the oath of office with his wife, Lady Bird, and Jacqueline Kennedy by his side.

I learned that day that the Constitution really works. A little more than an hour after the assassination of President Kennedy, the awesome powers of the presidency were transferred, peacefully, briefly, solemnly. Lyndon Johnson swore the same oath, spoke the same words, as did George Washington 174 years earlier, precisely, according to the design of fifty-five men who wrote it all down on a piece of parchment in Philadelphia in 1787. God, I find that miraculous.

I learned that politics need not be sordid nor soiled by dissemblers and hypocrites. Politics is exciting, worthy, an honorable enterprise deserving of the best that the best can offer, exacting from public men and women a firm conviction always to do what is right on behalf of the people they have by solemn oath sworn to serve.

Take Senator David Boren as your exemplar and you will do what is right to do. You will feel the pride that comes from public service, indeed it can become the summertime of your life. It certainly was mine. Politics can become all of that and more if enough young folks like you do not remain aloof or casual or disinterested.

I learned that it is the educated, civilized man and woman like you who, in the words of Edith Hamilton, are best fitted to confront life's changes, challenges, and angers and to meet them all with versatility and grace. That is, if you don't sit on the sidelines or turn a blind eye to your country's needs, secure in your own fat supply of stock options.

I learned that the movie world rocks and rolls. A number of folks in television and movies may seem a bit wacky and some off the wall, but none of them is dull. I find dullness to be the one sin for which there is no expiation. Everywhere on this wracked and weary planet the American movie captivates audiences in all countries, of all creeds and cultures. Which is why I am continually enticed by and in awe of actors, directors, writers, producers, craftsmen, most of whom are genuinely gifted artists whose works will endure. They are among America's most valuable assets. Maybe one day some of you will join that creative community. And I will be there to welcome you!

Now comes my final thought. And the noise I hear is heavy grateful breathing.

How many of you have seen Saving Private Ryan? *Steven Spielberg's extraordinary film may be the greatest epic of war ever filmed.*

You remember the opening scene in the movie, don't you? Those young men boiling out of landing crafts, wading through the rough waves of a rolling sea, accepting rifle, mortar, and machine gun fire from deadly assassins in the bunkers above the beach who cut them down in the water and on the sand.

Some time ago, when my son was about fifteen years old, a bit younger than most of you, I took him with me to visit Omaha Beach in the Normandy country of France. We stood on the bluff above the beach and gazed down on that sandy strip of land still absorbing the blood that flowed so freely on June 6, 1944, when the future of the free world was put in terrible peril.

Then we walked to the cemetery just above Omaha Beach. There, on land deeded by France to the United States, reside forever the bodies of 9,386 American fighting men. On a coverlet of green that stretches endlessly in elegant verdant splendor are marble crosses and Stars of David. They stand silently in serried ranks, row upon row upon row, as far as the eye can see. I dare any

American to look upon that outdoor cathedral of the brave and not weep.

I asked my son to inspect those mute markers, and read upon them the bland finalities that summed up so briefly the lives of those young-sters—name, rank, outfit, and the day of death. I say to you in this audience this day as I said to my son on that day, never forget that beneath that French earth, now American hallowed soil, lie the remains of boys, mostly between the ages of eigh-teen and twenty-four, a bit older than my son then, but your age today. Never forget that the end of life came to those lads before their lives could be lived.

How lucky you are. The future ahead of you is bright with promise. You young men and women have the opportunity as the result of your peerless education at the University of Oklahoma to reach to the highest point to which your ability, your resolve, and your ambition can soar. There are no barriers, no barricades, no bunkers to bar your way. You will be able to make your own choices, to read, watch, listen, and speak your mind as you see fit, for no one has the power to interrupt the way you want to live.

This, my young friends, is the gift of freedom. It is a gift bought for you and paid for in blood and bravery.

It is a gift that allows you to live out your life in this free and loving land, never having to test your own courage to see how you would react when a dagger is at the nation's belly and death stares you in the face.

It is a gift wrapped in valor and unbelievable acts of individual heroism whose recounting has to shake the very foundations of your comprehension.

It is a gift springing from the discipline and daring of young boys who never turned back, who defined the word D-U-T-Y and died even as the definition rang out loudly along the edge of the sea running red with blood.

It is a gift and a debt you and my son can never repay.

I am now done. I hope you listened. I hope you heard. I hope you care.

The speech I delivered that commencement day was not the exact replica of the speech that was conveyed to the press later. (An important note: Never release your written speech to the press before you speak. Otherwise, reporters and everyone else will sit with head bowed over your pages, listening to you as they read, but not really observing you.) There were digressions as I spoke, after which I returned to my notes as best I could. I did not allow myself to be bothered by those momentary diversions. What I strained for was the essence of what I had prepared to say. Remember, your audience does not know when and where you are deleting or revising. (I recall that JFK's aides jokingly referred to him as a "textual deviant" because he often leaped out of the written speech to offer some sentence or two that came to him as he spoke.) The essential element is to establish a rapport with the audience, to keep them interested in what you are saying. If their attention seems to be wandering, it is not the audience's fault but rather your own. Sometimes I injected a stab at humor to reclaim their attention and then, having fixed their interest on the point I was trying to make, went forward with the main thought.

You will see that the notes below, the notes I used for this speech, are mere signal lights, to direct my own concentration to the idea in each particular paragraph I spoke. Remember, I read this speech some thirty times. I was totally, intimately familiar with the written text. What the notes offered me was a few words that immediately alerted my mind to the line or paragraph to follow. Again the magic of a truly successful, notes-only speech is in the preparation. I promise you, it works. All you do is supply the labor ahead of time.

When speaking from notes, do not allow yourself to be thrown by the fact that you have not memorized your speech verbatim. Let the signal lights guide

you. Don't fret if you wander off the point, if you momentarily forget your original phrasing, which you thought to be so delightfully designed. Don't panic. Keep moving, and if the thought has fled your mind totally, go on to the next point in your notes, making as graceful a transition as you can muster. Keep in mind that the audience understands that you are speaking without the support of a full text and they will be tolerant most of the time. Keep looking at the audience, glancing at your notes only when you need to refresh your memory.

I memorized the first two paragraphs and the last two short paragraphs. That has large asset value. When you begin your speech you don't have to refer to notes. At the ending paragraph, speak directly to the audience. Your climax ought to be an interlocking embrace between you and your audience with no distractions, not even a glance down, however fleeting, at your notes.

Here are my actual notes for the speech, "The Gift of Freedom":

> *lived long enough . . .*
> *no one indispensable—light in the WH never goes out*
>   *story of Dallas*
> *Const. really works. LBJ spoke same words, same*
>   *oath*

Find that miraculous
Politics not sordid, soiled—
Honorable enterprise
Boren your exemplar
Edith Hamilton quote
Movie industry rocks & rolls
Final thought: Saving Private Ryan
Young men boiling out of landing craft . . .
Took my son at 15 to Omaha Beach . . . still absorbing blood
Cemetery—9,386 Americans
Marble crosses and stars of David
Inspect mute markers
How lucky you are . . . no barriers, barricades, bunkers
Gift of freedom
Gift—paid for in blood and bravery
Gift—allows you to live your life—dagger at nation's belly
Gift—wrapped in valor
Gift—springing from discipline, daring
Gift—can never repay

Speaking from notes, particularly from no more than two sheets of paper, allows you to approach the rostrum virtually empty-handed, relieving your audience of the notion that the speech you are about to deliver will be endless torture. There is, to an audience, something particularly welcome and gratifying in the sighting of a single sheet or two of written notes.

And they will sense, as you speak, that what you say is coming from the heart (a cliché to say that, yes, but it is true).

If you are a corporate officer talking to security analysts, or a city official addressing the chamber of commerce, the method of preparation is no different from that required by the treasurer of the local Rotary Club offering an accounting of the year's activities, or a soccer mom speaking to a citizens group about a local legislative proposition.

The preparation of your material, the careful making of notes, the practice sessions you privately repeat will be the same no matter the environment of your speech. Speaking from notes is a learned craft, and anyone capable of sustained concentration and eager to make a good impression can do a good job with any audience.

Know your subject thoroughly. Write out the speech in full ahead of time. If you can't do that, at least write down the key points you want to cover and any figures you want to use. Put these down on paper in the order in which you want to deliver them. Write out your conclusion in full, and memorize it—then you will have the option of ending your speech at

**whatever point you consider it timely to conclude
simply by using your closing paragraph.**

───────

A further word about eye contact: As you speak, you
will find yourself gazing out at an audience—a blurred,
indefinable mass. The fact that you are gazing but not
seeing becomes readily apparent to those who are listening. So, pick out several individual people. Speak directly
to them. A woman in the front row: As you speak, talk
directly to her. Lock your eyes on hers. After a moment
or two, turn your head slowly to the other side. A balding
man in a blue shirt: Fix your eyes on him as you talk.
And so on.

The motive here is simple. When you talk directly to
a specific person, nervousness tends to fade, for you are
now in a one-on-one conversation—which is ordinary,
the way most of us talk. The incentive to shout or become
strident is now lessened. You are in a companionable situation, discussing your subject with someone who has
come to hear what you have to say and is according you
the compliment of sitting quietly while you talk. Moreover, you need not try to overpower, merely to persuade.
You do this every day—in your family life, in your business, as you shop and make inquiries.

The more you speak in public, the easier it will become
to fasten your attention on one person and try to interest
that person in what you are saying. After some practice,

you will be pleasantly surprised to find you can discourse with more facility when your eyes are making friends with individual people in your audience. You will be able to move from one person to another, not abruptly but easily. It is the required first step in gaining rapport, a figurative handshake.

Put it another way: If you were in your living room conversing with a group of your friends and you gazed above them as you spoke, never meeting anyone's eyes, virtually talking over their heads, would you consider yourself impolite? Or arrogant? Would your friends be annoyed by your apparent rudeness?

Speaking to numbers of people in a more formal setting doesn't diminish the need for civility. Be interested in them as human beings and not merely as stage props conveyed to the hall for your exercise in public speaking.

Here is some additional counsel for you. Oftentimes at large events, house lights are dimmed, and spotlights are used. In this landscape, the spotlight's glare will literally curtain off those seated in front of you. You will look into a sea of blackness. It is as if you are speaking in an ill-lit cavern to a faceless crowd. Therefore, always ask for the house lights to come up when you go to the rostrum. Now, the room is bathed in openness. You can see everyone. You can make contact with them. You can better win them over.

Lord Chesterfield, a witty observer of mores and manners, summed up the necessity for winning over an audience. He once wrote: "The manner of your speaking is full as important as the matter, as more people have ears to be tickled than understanding to judge."

Engage your audience by reaching out to them. As you speak, think that all who sit in front of you are your friends, with whom you will share something useful, valuable, or at least sufficiently attractive to absorb their attention for a few moments. If you are successful, you will have imparted a message that will be understood, retained, and even acted on.

Now, let's discuss the TelePrompTer, which has become to speakers what the life net is to trapeze artists. JFK and LBJ were the first presidents to use the TelePrompTer. Now it is used by every president, and can be found in just about every TV studio in every television station in the country. The TelePrompTer, grown quite sophisticated today, is simply your speech on rolling pages controlled by an operator backstage at a computer that allows the speech page to be lifted by light and mirrors to panes of glass in front of the speaker. The glass is transparent to the audience. They cannot see anything except a piece of glass with nothing on it. To the speaker, the speech in easy-to-read white on black letters, large enough to see with ease, is a written text, which, as mentioned earlier, the audience cannot see.

Business chieftains, television newspeople, and politicians find in them the grandest illusion possible in convincing audiences that the speaker is dancing on a tightrope with no safety net beneath him or her. Take an observant note of presidents, cabinet officers, business tycoons, TV anchors, and others whose performances are displayed on television. On a tight close-up the viewer does not know that the speaker, moving unhesitatingly with fluid sentences that parse, no stumbling, no fumbling, is getting divine guidance from the TelePrompTer. And that's exactly the impression one wants to fasten onto an audience.

If a TelePrompTer is available at whatever speaking assignment you have, use it. It is mightily helpful. But a cautionary note: If you have never used a TelePrompTer, don't fail to test it out before you speak. Before the meeting convenes, meet with the person who will operate the machine. Let him or her know how you will speak, that is, whether you will depart from your text from time to time or stick to it religiously. Then ask the machine operator to allow you to try out the first two or three pages of your speech, speaking from the rostrum with the TelePrompTer in action. Is the operator keeping up with you? Is the TelePrompTer at the right level for you? Sometimes there is just one TelePrompTer in front of you, sometimes one on either side of you. If there's just one, you must attempt to move your gaze from side to side, else you are forced to stare ahead, manacled to the words on the machine. With a little practice you can do this quite easily. If there are two TelePrompTers, one on your left and one on your right, make sure that you move your eyes to the center frequently, as you glide from the left TelePrompTer to the right and back again. Don't let your eyes get tethered to either TelePrompTer. Let your eyes cover the entire audience as you read from the prompter, first to the left TelePrompTer, then go to the center of the room— that is, disconnect from the TelePrompTer for a few words—and then to the right TelePrompTer.

So, if you have never used a prompter, test it out, get as used to it as you can before you speak.

On a personal note: If I have truly mastered my preparation of a speech, if I am going to deliver it without notes or with notes and I find out some days in advance that a TelePrompTer is on the rostrum, I always ask for a long cord on the mike, or have myself wired to a cordless mike. That way I can step around the rostrum and very obviously avoid the TelePrompTer. Why waste all that preparatory labor if everyone thinks the TelePrompTer is riding shotgun for you?

CHAPTER FIVE

The Comic Line

*When—and When Not—to Be
Funny*

You walk near quicksand when you try to be funny. Uttering a comic line, telling a story that you hope will get a laugh, infusing wit into a serious subject: These are hazardous ventures for the speaker who is not by nature and inclination a humorous person.

The Earl of Louderdale, well known for his awkward ability to spoil any good story, once asked permission of celebrated Irish playwright Richard Brinsley Sheridan to repeat a funny story that Sheridan had recounted to a group of friends.

Sheridan replied: "My dear fellow, I must be careful of what I say in your presence, for a joke in your mouth is no laughing matter."

That anecdote contains the kernel of some very wise advice. It is accepted dogma that one should begin a speech, any speech, with some kind of funny story. I recoil when I remember otherwise charming, sensible, and honest friends of mine who, on rising to speak, begin by trying to regale their audience with a story calculated to loosen up the assembly. More often than not the story has little relevance to what follows, and it is usually presented with the skill one might expect of a butcher performing open-heart surgery.

Humor is a delicate animal. When it is trotted out by anyone who in normal social intercourse is not noted for it, it becomes a shaggy beast hunkered down in the pathway of an otherwise sensible talk.

Art Buchwald is one of those rarities, a genuinely funny man. He can recite portions of the Gospel according to Saint Mark and convulse his audience. He relies on a combination of speaking style and carefully formed prose tailored to his own unique personal gifts. He simply cannot be duplicated. Art had composed a speech for a famous fellow to give at the Gridiron Dinner in Washington, D.C. Art hosted a pre–Gridiron dinner at his home the night before the event. At this small gathering of no more than twenty friends, Art delivered the speech he had written for the famous fellow who sat next to Art. It was hilarious. All of us, veteran Washington observers, seasoned pros all, doubled over in laughter. The verdict was unanimous: "The famous fellow will crock 'em tomorrow night."

The next evening, some fifteen hundred white-tied members of the Establishment—publishers from all over the country, government officials of high station, Supreme Court justices, political and business captains, congressmen, senators, ambassadors, White House aides, military brass, reporters, and the president and vice president of the United States—were sitting chockablock in the Statler Hilton Hotel when the famous fellow rose to his feet.

I nudged a friend sitting next to me and whispered, "You're going to hear something that will put you in the aisles." My friend nodded appreciatively; he hadn't been in the aisles all evening.

Then the famous fellow began to speak. He spoke well. The vowels were formed with grace. The sentences parsed. But the humor—where the hell was the humor? The lines that in Buchwald's mouth had driven us to helpless laughter the night before were now echoing hollowly through the hall with nary a chuckle. The singsong, undulating comic rhythms of Art Buchwald were replaced by patrician tones marching in pedestrian ranks. The exquisite Buchwald timing was nowhere to be found. The result was a large, numbing bomb, which set a record for the longest period of mute silence ever in any Gridiron Dinner and retired the trophy for Most Boring (which is why I choose not to name the actual name of the "famous fellow").

This story confirms Sheridan's maxim: What is hilarious from one person's mouth may be no laughing matter in another's.

Humor, however, is an attractive asset. Even those of

us who are not professional comedians should be able to learn how to repeat a comic tale.

Timing is the key to a successful comic line. But achieving proper timing (think "pause") is not something that can be treated casually. What you are aiming for is the abolition of stiffness and stuffiness. You are searching for an effortless manner—and a skillful handling of the punch line. And, if there are certain words that trigger the final effect, they should be carefully rehearsed, over and over again. Timing means using the "pause," delicately, easily. Which is why a funny story should be practiced as diligently as an entire speech.

Let's take an example.

Say you are an accountant or an economist or a professor and you are speaking to a gathering of your own kind. You can tailor this story to fit your audience.

It could go something like this (if you are an accountant):

I am constantly reminded by those who use our services that we often turn out a ton of material on the subject but we do not always give our clients something of value.

A balloonist high above the earth found his balloon leaking and managed to land on the edge of a green pasture. He saw a man in a business suit approaching, and very happily said: "How good it is to see you. Could you tell me where I am?"

The well-dressed man replied: "You are standing in a wicker basket in the middle of a pasture."

The story is told without trying to be an actor or a comedian. It is being told straight. Now you are nearing the punch line, so you must take care that you don't ruin the effect by stumbling over the next few words—no problem if you have prepared yourself, practiced enough.

"Well," said the balloonist, "you must be a CPA."

The man was startled. "Yes, I am, but how did you know that?"

"That's easy," said the balloonist, "because the information you gave me was very accurate [now, the slight pause—a bare second] and absolutely useless."

This story isn't a bell-churner but it has several assets to give it bulk: It is relevant to the audience. It contains enough self-deprecating truth in it to be appreciated by the audience as not totally without foundation. And, finally, it has a succinct punch line.

It is the pause, the two-three-second hesitation between the speaking of one sentence and the beginning of another that can become a speaker's high moment. The skillful use of the pause in a speech can, with practice, become as useful a tool as you can employ.

Remember Jack Benny's classic comedy routine in which a mugger approaches him, sticks a gun in his face, and snarls, "Your money or your life."

Benny stands silent in his trademark pose, one hand under his chin, the other under his elbow.

The audience, well aware of his comic reputation as a cheapskate, begins to chuckle. Benny has not said a word. He merely stares. The laughter builds.

The mugger snarls again: "Did you hear what I said? Your money or your life."

And Benny, exasperated by the interruption, replies (after a pause): "I'm thinking, I'm thinking!"

The laughter explodes. Jack Benny was the master craftsman of the pause, the silence that can become an art form in itself.

Remember the pause: Just before you deliver a punch line, or, in a more serious vein, when you want to emphasize a concluding point or make a special impression on your audience . . . pause.

Though it might not mean much to David Letterman or Eddie Murphy, appreciative laughter in response to a funny story has a magical, relaxing effect on a nonprofessional speaker. He or she has gained some minor intimacy with the audience and, feeling a little more self-confident, will move into the meat of the speech with a touch more assertion than if the anecdote had, like a flightless dodo, refused to take off from the rostrum.

Adlai Stevenson wore the mantle of humor with more assurance and greater facility than almost any public man I have ever heard (with the possible exception of Hubert Humphrey).

I recall I once heard him speak in New Jersey to an overflowing crowd of high-powered businessmen, the loftiest industrial commanders of the nation, 99 percent of whom had gleefully voted against him twice and eagerly awaited a third chance to thumb him down.

Stevenson rose, cheery, paunchy, half-smiling. His first words captured this hostile crowd: "Mr. Chairman, I am grateful to be with you and to see in this audience so many of my friends—[pregnant pause]—and none of my supporters!"

Laughter and then applause greeted the former presidential candidate, and the rest of the speech was hospitably received.

Humor is even more effective when it is encased within a speech, not as a separate story but as part of the fabric of the prose.

Shortly after his inauguration, President Kennedy addressed a hall full of press and congressmen at a large gathering in Washington. High on the list of mistakes and poor judgments the new young president was accused of was his selection of his brother Robert, whose legal and court experience was practically nil, to be attorney general.

How did Kennedy deal with this matter? After a few quips to loosen up his audience, he turned to his brother, also on the rostrum, and said: "There's been some criticism of me for selecting my brother to be attorney general. I don't see anything wrong with my trying to give him some legal experience—[pause]—before he goes out to the private practice of law."

Whatever objections were souring the minds of those who listened, they were now mollified by this elegant self-deprecatory shot that, for the time being, silenced the critics. Those close to the president observed, however, that the new attorney general might have felt the humor was not so self-deprecatory, since the butt of the joke was Robert, not John. Nonetheless, the president knew precisely what he was doing.

Eppie Lederer, better known as Ann Landers, spoke to a group in Washington, D.C., seriously discussing modern assaults on the nerve ends of society—those concerns and fears that overwhelm all families, including the prospect of crime in the streets. In the middle of her recitation of dismal statistics Mrs. Lederer paused. "The fact is," she deadpanned, "that in Washington it takes steel nerves to be a neurotic."

The juxtaposition of uncongenial truth with a creative comic line brought the audience alive. It made the acceptance of surly fact a bit more appealing.

Often there is an opportunity to rise at a dinner party and toast the guest of honor. In Washington the after-dinner toast is something of a tribal rite, as much a part of the dinner gathering as the cocktail and the soufflé. Dinner toasts have only one unvarying rule: brevity.

When Henry Kissinger was the secretary of state he hosted a dinner for the Chinese ambassador to the United States in Beverly Hills, California. The great of Hollywood were present, as well as a cadre of Chinese officials, only one of whom spoke English. This gentleman was seated just behind the ambassador, whispering into his ear the arcane speech of the American guests.

Among the famous movie stars at the table was Kirk Douglas. When Kirk rose to honor his host, he had the mischievous thought of testing the resourcefulness of the interpreter with a one-line toast. He smiled widely, lifted his glass, looked firmly at the ambassador, and said: "I lift my glass to Henry Kissinger, who is as American as"—ever so slightly, a pause—"apple strudel."

The Chinese ambassador cocked his eye toward his link with the English language, but alas, the interpreter gulped, hesitated, and then poured a torrent of words into the weary ear of his chief. The ambassador nodded briefly, turned to look at his aide, who murmured again, then turned back to Kirk and nodded appreciatively.

Kirk later said to me, "I always wondered what the hell that interpreter said to the ambassador."

Kirk had spoken briefly, and he had said enough to lengthen his one sentence in English into a thousand words of Chinese. Damned inscrutable, these Americans.

Sometimes you have to be careful about humor. It should not offend those to whom you speak. For example, I am not sure I didn't go a little overboard one evening when I was speaking to a group of cruise ship operators. After heralding the fact that cruise ship vacations were big business (to which they nodded appreciatively) and citing other facts well known to them, I casually injected, "But as for me, I heartily dislike sea travel. Not only is being on a ship like being in prison, but there is the added possibility that you may drown."

A slight hesitation as the audience pondered that a few seconds, then steadily rising laughter. I did not inform them of the further truth that I had stolen the line, with minimal alterations, from Dr. Samuel Johnson—I didn't want to burden them with too many footnotes.

The best humor is spontaneous humor, not storytelling or gags, but humor derived from the material of the speech or built on something that has been said or done on the occasion of the speech.

This means you should listen carefully to all that has been said before you rise to speak. Drawing humor from the moment is a fine art, but it can be learned if you listen attentively. You can't tell ahead of time what you may be able to draw from previous speakers, but often it can be a crucial part of what you say later.

Here is one example: Some time ago, I was asked to be the speaker at the annual banquet staged by Covington and Burling, one of Washington's largest and most prestigious law firms. Two hundred or so lawyers and their spouses and friends gathered to enjoy themselves (and in a big firm like Covington and Burling, some were meeting each other for the first time). It is an evening in which the speaker, if he is to survive the next day's comments, strives to avoid being long-winded and blowsy. Not being a lawyer, I had nothing technical to convey except some observations about Washington itself.

I was introduced by a brilliant young partner of the firm, a Yale Law School graduate. In his introductory remarks, he was slyly amusing, offering some in-house jokes about his associates, which drew appreciative chuckles from his audience. I listened intently to his presentation.

When my turn came I rose and began:

> I am not sure I can follow the humorous sallies constructed by the chairman, a graduate of the Yale Law School. Anticipating such a prelude, I

consulted with a number of my friends more expert than I in examining the entrails of Yale graduates. The summary of what they told me is, "Just remember one thing: There is no such thing as a Yale lawyer with humor. Odd, maybe; strange, usually; rich, always; but humorous— [pause]—never."

The audience seemed to love it, including the Yale Law School alumni. Some of them even managed a tight, thin slice of a smile.

Some years back, I was one of several on a rostrum before a large assembly of Washingtonians gathered to "roast" Art Buchwald. Also scheduled to speak were George Stevens, Jr., cochairman of the American Film Institute and son of the distinguished movie director; and Joseph Califano, the former secretary of Health, Education, and Welfare, who had been unceremoniously sacked from that post by President Carter.

Mr. Califano made a delightful talk toasting and roasting Art, except that he inadvertently used a line I was myself poised to deliver.

When I was introduced, before I launched into my own diatribe I greeted the audience and then turned to Califano: "I am a bit vexed because Joe Califano just stole one of my best lines. Now I know why President Carter fired the 'sumbitch.' " The crowd roared in appreciative laughter. Because I had listened to Califano, I had been able to forge a fairly good riposte—which the audience knew had not been in my mind when the program began.

Use the time before you are called on to speak to open your ears and listen. There is almost always something said or done in those moments that you can utilize to spark your presentation, to give it immediacy—most assuredly a sharp arrow to fit to your bow.

Humor is also more appreciated when it is least expected.

Some years ago, at Twentieth Century-Fox studios, a reception was held for Arlene (Mrs. Alan) Alda. Arlene is a bright, charming lady who, with unique confidence, bears the burden of being the wife of a celebrated movie and television star. She is seldom before the public, since her principal task has been that of wife and mother of three daughters. But on this evening there was a jubilant celebration of the publication of her new book, *On Set*, containing photographs she had taken of the making of her husband's films. She wrote the text also, surehanded prose about the inside of moviemaking.

Arlene was introduced and came to the microphone: a small, smiling, obviously happy lady.

The audience expected a serviceable few words, and was ready to applaud civilly and appreciatively. The food had been delicious and there were celebrities present to satisfy the stargazers.

She began: "I am not very good before an audience. I usually leave that to my husband. Indeed, I was quite nervous when I was to be interviewed by Tom Brokaw. A young lady came in with a clipboard, bustling with energy and some hesitation. She came up to me and said: 'Are you the person who is against spanking?' I said, 'No, but I would be glad to sign the petition.' "

The audience, surprised by the sudden splash of humor, exploded into laughter.

But she wasn't through: "I am always asked how it feels to be Mrs. Alan Alda, wife of a famous director, writer, star, and sex symbol! After the tour we put together all my answers to this question, asked about a hundred times, and the result of the compilation was that I was a pathological liar."

Again, the audience screamed its delight. And then: "On tour we stopped in Denver and dined with Marvin and Barbara Davis. [Mr. Davis, a Denver oil billionaire, at one time owned Twentieth Century-Fox.] When I told the Davises of the some thirty or forty cities on my itinerary, Barbara Davis looked at me curiously and said: 'Who's going to do your hair?' "

After this, it was the settled conclusion of the assembly that Arlene was the star of the Alda family. Her speech

was totally professional, totally relevant, and quite un-
expected.

One wouldn't describe the late Nikita Khrushchev as
one of the great humorists, but he possessed a cunning
peasant wit dug out of the ancient soil of Mother Russia
herself. Khrushchev made a famous 1966 secret speech.
This address to the Supreme Soviet contained a stunning
compilation of Stalin's brutal crimes and marked the first
time anyone in the Politburo had the temerity to go public
with that lamentable catalog. After Khrushchev had finished he responded to questions, all of them written out
on paper and handed up to the speaker.

One question was, "Since you knew Stalin was a mon-
ster, why did you work so closely with him?"

Khrushchev read the question and, without a moment's hesitation, replied, "For the same reason the com-
rade who sent up this question did not sign it."

Unhappily, we have no commentary on the reaction
of the audience.

It is one thing to plan one's sallies in advance, it is
quite another to fling a piece of barbed prose even as the
oratorical muskets are firing. In my judgment perhaps the
finest example of spontaneous wit is the instant response
of Harold Wilson, former prime minister of Great Britain
but at the time leader of the Labour Opposition, in a
debate in the Commons.

Duncan Sandys, the Tory minister of defense (and
Churchill's son-in-law), had just spoken on the subject of

the Blue Streak missile, which was apparently unable to get off the ground after ten failed attempts, but still was part of the British defense arsenal. When Sandys had completed his rebuttal to critics of the Blue Streak, he then called for the Commons to approve an additional several million more pounds to try an eleventh time. Wilson rose quickly to his feet, one hand grasping his coat lapel, his eyes fastened on the defense minister.

"We all know," he began, "why Blue Streak was kept on although it was an obvious failure. It was to save the face of the minister of defense. We are, in fact, looking at the most expensive face in history. It is true that Helen of Troy's face may have launched a thousand ships—[an elegant pause]—but at least they were operational!"

The House broke up in huge laughter. Sandys could find no suitable rejoinder. He sat down, dejected, defeated. Wilson's missile attack on Sandys was a huge triumph. Did he construct that magnificent thrust ahead of time? Or did he compose it at the moment? I don't know. But I want to believe Wilson rose to the occasion without prior design, flying to the highest point to which the cutting oratorical blade can rise.

Sir Winston Churchill was an admitted master of the literate karate chop. In a debate with Austen Chamberlain, half-brother of Neville Chamberlain (Britain's prime minister at the infamous Munich meeting with Hitler), Churchill looked squarely at Chamberlain and said in mock sorrow, "The honorable gentleman has always played the game—[a slight pause]—and has always lost it."

It was the same Churchill who devastated the monkish Sir Stafford Cripps with one sentence: "He has all the virtues I dislike and none of the vices I admire."

Writers in the ancient classics reported humor readily at hand. Alcibiades was telling Pericles how Athens should be governed and Pericles was more than a little vexed at the young lad's effrontery.

"Alcibiades," the great Pericles admonished him, "when I was your age, I talked just about the way you are now talking." Whereupon Alcibiades smiled and retorted, "How I would have enjoyed knowing you, Pericles, when you were at your best."

Thomas Reed, the famed Czar Reed, speaker of the house at the turn of the century, once listened to Theodore Roosevelt expound at length on some subject in which Roosevelt made it patently clear that he was both expert and right.

Reed wearily lifted himself to his feet and said, "Theodore, if there is one thing more than another for which I admire you, it is your original discovery of the Ten Commandments."

It has been written (and while this response may be apocryphal, I yearn to believe it is true) that Voltaire was approached by a minor historian whose latest book Voltaire was prevailed upon to read through the importunings of intermediaries. When the historian chided Voltaire for his failure to comment, Voltaire quickly replied: "A historian has many duties. Allow me to remind you of two which are important. The first is not to slander; the second is not to bore. I can excuse you for neglect of the first because few will read your work. However, I cannot forgive you the second, for I was forced to read what you had written."

If I had a choice, I would have enjoyed listening to John Randolph of Roanoke, who was President Thomas Jefferson's floor leader in the House of Representatives, later senator from Virginia, and a cobra-tongued orator whose vituperative wit caused other public men to shrink from him in debate. He brought malice to its most poisonous levels and did it with a wit unequaled by any other parliamentarian in the early days of the Republic (or arguably today as well).

A brave but inadequate lancer who rose to joust with Randolph was a certain Philomen Beecher, congressman from Ohio. Randolph tolerated for a while Beecher's interruptions of "Previous question, Mr. Speaker," but when this had happened a number of times, Randolph finally turned a baleful glance on the noisy member.

"Mr. Speaker," Randolph said, "in the Netherlands, a mall of small capacity, with bits of wood and leather, will in a few minutes construct a toy that will, with the pressure of a finger and thumb, cry 'Cuckoo, cuckoo!' With less ingenuity, and with inferior material, the people of Ohio have made a toy that will, without much pressure, say 'Previous question, Mr. Speaker!'"

Amid gales of congressional laughter, Philomen Beecher slunk out of the chamber and out of history.

There is a contemporary sound to Randolph's wit. In a debate over an expensive appropriations bill, Randolph spoke in favor of economy and ended his remarks (all without notes, I must add) with this shot: "That most delicious of all privileges . . . spending other people's money."

As the senator from Virginia, Randolph listened to Missouri senator Thomas Hart Benton's filibuster for four solid days. When the filibuster had ended, Randolph rose and commented dryly: "I must remind my colleagues that Senator Benton's speech lasted one day longer than the French Revolution of 1830."

The melding of brain and tongue was so swift in Randolph that no one could be certain of his retort nor how lethal would be its explosion. He peppered two members of the House with one shot when he said about Robert Wright and John Rea that the House of Representatives contained two curious juxtapositions: "A Wright always wrong and a Rea without light."

One time a new member came to the House, elected to fill out the term of a dear friend of Randolph's who had died suddenly. The new member immediately began, with more courage than good sense, to cut up Randolph on the House floor. Randolph bided his time, until one afternoon discussion turned to a bill in which Randolph's late friend had had a keen interest.

Said Randolph, looking with grave disapproval at the new member, "This bill has lost much in the death of my dear friend, whose seat, alas, still remains vacant."

Before Martin Van Buren became president, he crossed Randolph in debate. The Virginian arose from his seat to comment on Van Buren: "He is a man who habitually rows to his object with muffled oars."

The largest talents of the Congress were not immune to Randolph's peculiar moods. He considered John Calhoun a man mad with lust for war. He never forgave or forgot Calhoun's stand as one of the war hawks who pushed the United States into the War of 1812, which Randolph opposed with all the fervor he could summon— which was quite a lot.

When Calhoun was vice president under John Quincy Adams, Randolph once began a speech in the Senate with these words: "Mr. Speaker, I mean Mr. President of the Senate and would-be President of the United States, which God in His infinite mercy avert."

Nonplussed, Calhoun was struck with silence, which was, by historical precedent, the proper way to confront Randolph.

In the history of speechmaking, there is one grand master, Benjamin Disraeli, who late in his life (at age sixty-three for one year, and then again at seventy) became prime minister of England. (The following is extracted from *The Bitter Taste of Glory,* a book I wrote about great political leaders.)

On the floor of the Commons, Disraeli was master. He was a professional, totally in charge of the complex procedures of the House and instantly knowledgeable of the labyrinth of debate. He battled all the great orators of the day, unattended by aides or colleagues, with either his skill or his courage, never faltering even in ill health, always feared, often hated, never ignored.

Early in his career, he took on Sir Robert Peel and destroyed him. It was done deftly, precisely, and with a surgeon's unerring eye for the right place to apply the scalpel.

It began rather inauspiciously. Peel rose to cut down this foppish young innocent. He used as his saber some lines uttered by a predecessor, Canning. The lines were apt and effective. But it was a dangerous game that Peel played, for he had earlier done in Canning in the Commons which Canning's words had so eloquently condemned.

Disraeli did not reply at first. A few days went by. Then Disraeli spoke quietly, to protest against the system of appealing to the loyalty of the Tories in order to make them vote for Whig measures.

It is valuable to give Disraeli's reply, for no one can capture the luxuriant shatter of the retort without the actual words. Listen to Disraeli:

> The right honourable gentleman [Peel]
> caught the Whigs bathing and walked away

with their clothes. He has left them in the full enjoyment of their liberal position and he himself a strict conservative of their garments. [The House laughed uproariously. Peel sat somber.]

If the right honourable gentleman may find it sometimes convenient to reprove a supporter on his right flank, perhaps we deserve it. I for one am quite prepared to bow to the rod, but really, if the right honourable gentleman, instead of having recourse to obloquy, would only stick to quotation, he may rely on it, it would be a safer weapon. It is one he always wields with the hand of a master; and when he does appeal to any authority, in prose or verse, he is sure to be successful, partly because he never quotes a passage that has not previously received the meed of parliamentary approbation, and partly and principally because his quotations are so happy.

The right honourable gentleman knows what the introduction of a great name does in debate—how important are its effects and occasionally how electrical. He never refers to any author who is not great and sometimes who is not loved, Canning for example. That is a name never to be mentioned I *am sure in the House of Commons without emotion. We all admire his genius. We all, at least most of us, deplore his untimely end. And we all sympathize with him in his fierce struggle with supreme prejudice and sublime mediocrity—with inveterate foes and with candid friends. The right honourable gentleman may be sure that a quotation from such an authority will always tell. Some lines, for example, upon friendship written by Mr. Canning and quoted by the right honourable gentleman. The theme, the poet, the speaker—what a felicitous combination! Its effect in debate must be overwhelming; and I am sure, if it were addressed to me, all that would remain would be for me thus publicly to congratulate the right honourable gentleman not only on his ready memory, but on his courageous conscience.*

The House was in an uproar. It was a stunning achievement. Disraeli had hoisted Peel on Canning's words. Peel sat hunched in his seat, quiet, breathing heavily, deeply provoked, but determined not to reveal it, and deeply hurt, hurt beyond measure that this upstart should be so savage, so gaily malignant to the prime minister.

Some time later he attacked Peel again, even more cruelly. He spoke with telling effect, and the last twenty minutes of his speech were rapid-fire shots of invective and deadly sarcasm.

He described how the Peelites, "like the Saxons confronting Charlemagne were converted in battalions and baptized in platoons." He hit Peel savagely for his vacancy of mind and his use of other people's ideas. "His life has been one long appropriation clause. He is a burglar of others' intellect. There is no statesman who has committed political larceny on so large a scale." It was the most cruelly discomforting day of Peel's career. One month later, he was thrown out of office. Disraeli had pulled the great man down with words dipped in curare.

We are more polite today, at least in the clubby atmosphere of the cloakroom, the stump, and the TV studio. But the absence of ceremonial verbal assault may be due more to the diminution of the art of lethal reply than concern for the other fellow's feeling. The format of opposition today has been drained of any style. It is mostly formless, noisy, rowdy, and, if a good phrase has surfaced, it has gotten lost in the cluttered din from which it came.

Pilfering is socially acceptable among speakers. Stealing good stories from those who are rich in the creative gift of laughter is an unpunishable, even fashionable, oratorical felony.

The irrepressible John Randolph, whose wit we have already examined, was the source of a bit of borrowing by a twentieth-century member of the U.S. Senate.

Once Randolph bore in on a hapless colleague with the statement: "His mind is like a parcel of land, poor to begin with and rendered more barren by too intensive cultivation."

That nugget lay glistening but unnoticed in the *Congressional Record* for a long time. Then in 1919, almost ninety years after Randolph died, Sen. Thaddeus Caraway of Arkansas stood on the Senate floor to bang away at the patrician senator from Massachusetts, Henry Cabot Lodge: "I have long heard of the reputation for wisdom and wit of the senator from Massachusetts, but his speech today has convinced me that his mind is like the land of his native state, barren by nature and impoverished by cultivation."

There were many that day who were astonished at the spontaneous wit of Senator Caraway. Few of them knew that somewhere in the recesses of Caraway's mind was that classic Randolph line, which he had no doubt read and retained to skewer Henry Cabot Lodge. Ah, to possess the "spontaneous" retort!

The ability to forge a kinetic answer to an unanticipated question is remarkably valuable. The skill to do this usually comes with experience, and an inner instinct.

At a Hewlett Packard employees' meeting in 2000, Carly Fiorina, HP's CEO, one of the few women at the top of a Fortune 500 company, was confronted with this abrupt question, which she could not have foreseen: "What keeps you up at night?" A very unlikely question and one that, I daresay, would confound any CEO who tried to come up with a cogent and believable answer. Fiorina did. She swiftly responded: "Time, because time is not on any of our sides. In this technology-driven world, the future is now. Seconds tick by and it is too late." Compact, incisive, to the point. Give her a grade of A.

Steve Case, chairman of the huge media/Internet enterprise, AOL/TimeWarner, put it another way when he spoke at a large gathering: "You know the song 'What a Difference a Day Makes'? In our business the song we sing is more like, 'What a Difference a Nanosecond Makes.' " Again, blending popular culture into an easily understood maxim. Well done, Mr. Case.

In my judgment, the very best public speaker in the American business community is Warren Buffett, the fabled chairman and CEO of Berkshire-Hathaway Corporation. To give you some idea of the seismic economic success of Buffett's investment wizardry consider this: If you had invested $10,000 in Berkshire in 1965, the year of its founding, your investment today would be worth some $51 million! If you had put that $10,000 in Buffett's partnership, which he created in 1956, and later folded it into Berkshire-Hathaway, it would be worth today some $300 million! As some would say, that's serious money.

Buffett's great gift is that he operates on a rostrum, or anywhere else, without notes or text (though he does infrequently use PowerPoint computer presentations). He can offer esoteric economic and market information to his audience in plain, unadorned language, which in turn produces a magical clarity. But his largest asset—which is invariably absent from just about every other high-stationed business executive's public performance—is his uncanny ability to weave into the economic disquisition blazes of wit and humor. No joke-teller he, not at all. His humor springs from throwaway lines, which connect to whatever it is he is saying.

Example: At the July 2001 Allen and Company business conference in Sun Valley, attended by a roster of lordly moguls from American commerce and industry, the Internet, Silicon Valley, movie studios, and TV networks, as well as investment gurus who manage over $2 trillion in funds, and the president of Mexico, Buffett took the stage and mesmerized an audience that is not easily stirred. He spoke about the history of ups and downs in the stock market. In the midst of deploying statistics that might have blurred the interest of any crowd, he injected casually, "These numbers are confirmed by the actuaries." Now, a finely honed pause, and then, "As a matter of fact when I was young I wanted to be an insurance actuary, but I didn't have enough charisma for the job." Wow! He had to wait for the laughter to die away.

If you find yourself speaking in public several times a year—in business or in conferences or at conventions or your community service club—begin to keep a journal of lines, sentences, stories, retorts you have read or heard. You will find this a treasure trove when you have to rise to your feet. Oftentimes, as you gain more assurance through practice, you will find one of these proven "bell-ringers" (as an old professional speaker once termed them) springing out of your memory, and you will be able to toss it off as if you had coined it on the spot.

I keep a journal and have done so for many years. When I was very young I read a biography of Thomas Jefferson in which I learned that from the time Jefferson was in his twenties, he kept a Commonplace Book, in which he wrote down every phrase, sentence, or paragraph he admired in his reading. I do the same. Every time I find a line or two that I value in a book I underline it and later write it in my journal. Over the years I have accumulated a fat volume of some five hundred pages brimming over with words, sentences, paragraphs I have appreciated—stately prose, saucy lines, ironic sentences from great authors, as well as sprightly, venomous humor from antic wits. When I inscribe a quotation in my journal, I carefully note where I heard or read it and from whom. If the item is from a book, I include the author, the title of the book, and the page number, so I can always refer back to the original to see the context in which it was said or written.

Disregard books of quotations. Too often a quotation from *Bartlett's* sounds exactly as if you had lifted it. It lacks the verisimilitude of the original, and besides, I count ransacking a quotation book a form of cheating. If I haven't read it in a book or heard it from a speaker, I consider its use equivalent to peeking at the hidden cards in solitaire.

You will soon find such a detailed, personal journal or card index of memorable phrases quite helpful in adding a light and leavening touch to your written speeches. An apt line will spark your creative juices, allowing you to refine, rephrase, and redesign the words to fit your specific audience and occasion. Don't feel guilty at pilfering from the great writers of the past. Modern-day writers and speakers all do it. (Please, keep in mind I am not exalting plagiarism; I mean a few words or a phrase, no more. Moreover, you should cite the source of a long sentence or a paragraph.) Examples are plentiful of such literary shoplifting. In his last public statement, just before he died, Thomas Jefferson wrote "that the mass of mankind has not been born with saddles on their back nor a favored few, booted and spurred to ride them." What Jefferson, a great prose stylist in his own right, neglected to note was that he appropriated that phrase, in briefer form, from the final words spoken on the scaffold in mid-seventeenth-century England by Richard Rumbold, an activist hater of the divine rights of kings and their ilk, just before he was hanged: "I never could believe that Providence had sent a few men into the world booted and spurred to ride, and millions ready, saddled, and bridled to be ridden."

On March 20, 1933, President Franklin D. Roosevelt sent rivers of joy throbbing through the American public when at his inauguration he spoke the memorable words: "The only thing we have to fear is fear itself." Not publicized by FDR's speechwriter was the fact that some four hundred years earlier Sir Francis Bacon had written: "Nothing is to be feared except fear itself." So, go ahead, pilfer from the best, because the best always do it.

CHAPTER SIX

The Camera's Eye

How to Speak before Television Cameras

In a workaday world grown complicated, so choked with technological alternatives and head-splitting econometric riddles, no one who aspires to success in any profession can neglect the art of communication. The role of communicator has become dominant in the careers of businessmen, professors, union shop foremen, politicians, indeed anyone who must try to convince others of a point of view. Even when your forum is a PTA meeting or a nonprofit organization where policy is being discussed, you are more apt to be persuasive if you understand something about the delicate art of speaking to others.

It is not enough to be intellectual, gorged with facts, smart, competent in administration, or in designing strategy. You must be able to speak reasonably, believably, engagingly to those whose support is necessary to your

119

cause. Knowing all the facts is one thing. Imparting those facts to others so that they understand and are open to persuasion is quite another. When knowledge is out of joint with the communication of knowledge, one may as well be blathering in the wind.

Which is why the prime platform for communication is television. It is possible to say that, in public life, if you are not on television, you don't exist.

To say that television has transformed the art of speaking is to utter the cliché of the generation. Today the principal medium for the communication of knowledge, information, news—and persuasion—is television. Sooner or later in your life, the cameras may well be on you. There is no surer or more powerful charm you can carry than the ability to say easily and clearly what you believe and why you believe it, as you speak into a camera, its unblinking eye fastened on you with the tenacity of a pit bull.

But you must bear in mind that speaking before a television camera is not the same as speaking to an audience in a large room, an auditorium, a sports arena, whatever. It is totally different. Unless the speaker understands that difference, the quality of speaking suffers.

Television is intimate, almost as if those who watch and listen are seeing you through a microscope. Vocal inflections, facial expressions, even the color of your tongue and alignment of your teeth are magnified and intensified. Television is a gigantic communications force.

It is also a cruel arbiter, illuminating warts as well as wisdom.

———

The indispensable element of television speaking can be summed as follows: Be conversational, as if you were in a living room talking to a half-dozen people. This does not mean you cannot gesture or lift your voice on a declamatory note, but it does mean you need not raise your voice too many decibels in order to be heard. Your very whisper becomes gloriously (or otherwise) audible.

———

Try to keep your passions in check, for what in a large auditorium is reasonable and captivating can become grotesque, wildly ridiculous on a smallish TV screen. I am reminded of Molière's comment expressed in one of his plays that while men do not get upset over being called wicked, they do strenuously object to being made ridiculous.

Often nonprofessionals (even, alas, professionals) are so mesmerized by the all-engulfing eye of the camera that they lose touch with reality.

———

Try to forget the camera eye. In fact, one *must* forget the camera eye. If you don't, sooner or later

your tongue and mind will collide. Not a happy prospect. But don't worry. Just dismiss the camera from your thoughts. Speak as if you are in your living room.

─────

There are several ways to keep the camera eye from distracting you. If you are on a panel show, or having a conversation with a group, or in a one-on-one interview, concentrate on those to whom you are talking. Look them in the eye and speak as if you were chatting in your home.

The biggest distraction is when you are alone in a studio on a remote hook-up with someone in Los Angeles or New York or Atlanta, or wherever. Your only companion (other than the camera operator) is the Cyclopean eye of that damnable camera. Even professionals don't find this situation amenable. I personally find this setting inhospitable. In your loneliness the camera stares at you in its catatonic trance.

The key is to consider the camera as anything but a camera. Conceive it as a window or a two-way mirror, or pretend that someone you trust is sitting in front of you. Speak to that imaginary friend.

Whenever you are alone in a television studio facing the camera, there is usually some delay, interminable to anyone anxious and nervous, before you get the signal to begin. These are crucial seconds. Your throat may grow dry. You may even find yourself having difficulty swallowing. It happens to the hardiest professionals. One reason for it is the inconvenience of that impersonal round black eye of the camera, focused so steadily on you. It is a most discomfiting gaze. Have a drink of water and breathe smoothly, easily. Remember, this happens to everyone, not just you.

I think it useful, if the studio allows it (and few of them do so, but you may try suggesting it), to have someone, preferably one or two people, either friends of yours or studio technicians, stand slightly behind and around the camera. When your cue comes, and the red light that signals the "on" camera adds its baleful glow to the eye of the lens, talk to them. If they are grouped closely around the camera, you will not be diverting your own gaze too far to the left or right of the lens but will be able to talk to living people rather than the robotlike, sterile companion menacing your serenity.

The good news is the more you confront this situation, the easier it becomes. Try above all else to be natural. Listen to the questions asked you through your earphone and pretend you are in your living room talking to someone as you answer. If you truly concentrate on what is being asked and ready yourself for the answer, the camera's unblinking scrutiny will fade away.

I tried, endlessly and without success, to persuade President Johnson, when delivering a television speech from the Oval Office, always to seat a couple of his friends or his family cheek-by-jowl with the camera.

"Talk to them, Mr. President, not the camera. Let the camera eavesdrop on what you are saying, but speak directly to those seated next to the camera." LBJ did it his way.

But in truth, the camera viewed merely as eavesdropper becomes a lesser intrusion, a kind of bystander. It is so very much easier to speak naturally, warmly, even passionately, to folks you know than to a lens.

Don't panic if you feel an explosive anxiety just before you begin to talk. It is natural, and human. Keep in mind that you will be talking conversationally to people. Look them, not the camera, in the eye.

Again, preparation is the companion of success in any kind of speaking, including speaking on TV.

Know what you want to say. Don't worry about remembering precise phrasing, but know essentially the ideas you want to present. This means prior study. Think about what you will say at some length beforehand. When you are by yourself you might even speak aloud what you intend to say, always remembering that you probably will say it differently when you are before the camera. That is not important. Don't let memory frighten you because you don't have to memorize. Know the outline of what you intend to say. Sometimes, if there is sufficient advance notice, you can have a TelePrompTer beneath the camera lens to offer the security of the printed word to fall back on.

If you are on a question-and-answer show where others are going to query you, "moot court" your appearance. That is, do as lawyers do before they try a case, or as presidents of the United States do before appearing at a press conference: Try to figure out in advance the questions you think you will be asked. If the format of the program is known, it is a relatively simple proposition to predict many of the questions that will be put to you.

Before any press conference, all presidents sit with their advisers for several hours. The aides assume the roles of reporters and ask the most savage questions imaginable. The aides and the president go over, time and time again, those questions that intelligence gathering tells the White House are most likely to be posed. Aides ask questions in confrontational tones, trying to duplicate, insofar as it is possible, the actual press conference to come. The fact is, the "moot court" can be so venomous that the actual press conference oftentimes seems serene.

After each question, the president offers an answer. Then his aides explore and dissect his reply: Not quite right. Not really to the point. Then, the question again.

What about a question that the president really didn't want to answer, or that required him to reveal so much about his intentions or strategy that he would be boxed in, unable to make alternative moves? The solution would be to "fuzz up" the answer so that he could glide out of that minefield and land lightly on another query more easily handled. Fuzzing up doesn't mean lying, or even dancing around the turns, but simply keeping one's options open. In the LBJ White House we concentrated on these questions until the president was satisfied that his answer was pointed enough but not sufficiently revealing to impede his future actions. Note that a president never loses a press conference. He is in total command. If he truly doesn't want to answer the question, he can fuzz up or he can give an answer to a question that hasn't been asked. Then he can move to the next questioner to avoid the question, because one journalist never follows up on another journalist's question.

To be honest, this kind of hazy response does invite disaster. Often what we considered a reasonable answer didn't take with the press. On one occasion, we knew President Johnson would be asked about the removal of Henry Cabot Lodge as ambassador to Vietnam. The president had earlier determined that Lodge would be recalled and he had already asked General Maxwell Taylor to take his place. Taylor had agreed, and it was only a matter of waiting for the appropriate time to make the announcement. But Lodge had not yet been informed specifically, so it was agreed by all that this particular press conference was not the time to light that torch. How to maneuver? How to field the question we knew with absolute certainty would be asked?

The exchange went something like this. Question: "Mr. President, are you thinking about removing Ambassador Lodge and are you thinking now about a successor?"

LBJ, without breaking stride, answered, "No, I am not thinking about that at all. Next question."

Consider the Jesuitical logic of that answer, and the way it was asked. "Are you thinking about . . . ?" The president's answer was strictly correct and totally honest in his mind: No he wasn't thinking about that at all. He had already done it, so he wasn't thinking about it.

Several days later when the president did make the announcement, the press landed on him with bludgeons and meat axes. Credibility gap! President untruthful! Goddamn lie! These were some of the milder aspersions.

The president was genuinely upset. How on earth could he be libeled as being untruthful, when in fact he had answered honestly and correctly?

The White House staff gulped a few times, and we had to admit as we sat around grousing about press conspiracies that the press did have a point. But how else to handle it? That was a no-win situation, as we were armed with a feebly righteous sword, visibly rusted, which we brandished without much effect.

But there is a central truth to presidential press conferences that is, the president never loses a press conference. Why? Because he is in command. He can use or not use an opening statement. If he has a message he wants to convey to the voters, the opening statement gives him a pathway to voters' eyes and ears. If a question is offered him he really doesn't want to answer, he can fob it off and go on to the next questioner, who—and this has been a joy to every White House press secretary—won't follow up on the question of another journalist.

Television has reshaped the language and the rhythms of speech. Because time is so important in TV, thirty or forty seconds becomes a long time for one person to be on camera. If you are being interviewed briefly about a business decision, or about a discussion you've just had in a closed-door meeting, or any other situation where the exchange lasts about twenty seconds, design in your mind what you want to say, and say it compactly, and with as much color as possible.

Seasoned professionals in public life learn early that when a journalist sticks a microphone in front of your face the first priority is to be brief. The second priority is to say what you want to say and wish to have heard by the audience, in one to three sentences. The third priority is to try to add some color to what you say.

On network and local news shows, there is more material than can be used. It is the role of the editor to cull out the banal, the droning, the bulky, the inadequate, and to keep intact what is useful to the story and, importantly, adds sauce (whether laughter, sympathy, anger, grief, or other emotional component) to the segment. Therefore, if what you say is succinct and has heft, the chances are you will not end up on the cutting-room floor.

When the fifty-two American hostages returned from their imprisonment in 1981, one of the group who was particularly articulate on television was Bruce German. He was, by instinct, brief and pungent in expression. "Would you go back to Iran?" he was asked.

Without breaking stride, he answered, "Yeah, in a B-52." That segment of film hit every network and local news show. It was simply too good to be edited out.

I persistently advise my congressional friends to keep in mind this simple admonition: When leaving a committee hearing or a visit with the White House staff or whatever, he or she should head for the waiting cameras thinking about what he or she is going to say and trying to encapsulate it in a sentence. It is easier to do that if you think about how to put a "therefore" at the end of your first sentence and make "therefore" the beginning of your second and last sentence.

What's a "therefore"? Let me explain.

I enjoy telling my younger colleagues a story about Sam Rayburn, the powerful Speaker of the House in the Eisenhower and Kennedy years. Rayburn once had a momentary falling out with President Franklin D. Roosevelt (when Rayburn was merely a committee chairman). One of Rayburn's colleagues was going to visit FDR and Rayburn urged him to find out what the president thought about the controversy. The congressman obligingly agreed.

Later that day, the congressman visited Rayburn's office and said, "Now, when the president had me enter the Oval Office, I told him . . ." and he launched on an interminable recital of what he had said to FDR.

Finally Rayburn exploded: "I don't give a good goddamn about what you told FDR, but I damn sure want to know what Roosevelt told you!"

I tell this story with relish. So whenever some one of my colleagues or a lobbyist I have retained to visit an influential member of Congress embarks on a windy report, I blandly interrupt and say, "Remember Sam Rayburn? Therefore, therefore." What I mean is, get to the point: What did the member say to you? Therefore: What is your conclusion?

I counsel my congressional friends, when they know they are about to be asked questions by journalists, especially those with cameras, to have their "therefore" ready. For instance: "I just finished a twenty-minute meeting with the president." (And now the "therefore.") "I told the president that the base in Slippery Rock should not be closed if he truly cares about our national defense and the security of this country."

The congressperson (or senator) will surely be on the evening news that night if the subject is at all important, because (1) he specified with precision the presence of a juicy controversy, and (2) he said it so briefly no editor can fool with it.

Another way to assure yourself of a ten-second spot

on the networks is to put your "therefore" in an epigram-matic frame. No editor can resist keeping it inside the story.

A senator believes in more money for the armed forces. Leaving a hearing room where the defense budget is being debated, he wants to make clear his commitment to that cause. A mike is thrust under his mouth and the camera eye gapes at him.

QUESTION: "Senator, is the defense budget going to be increased?"

ANSWER: (The "therefore" up front and dressed in spice.) "If I have my way, it will. The world is on fire and all we did today was sit in there playing a broken fiddle."

The senator has made three points: (1) he is for a strong defense; (2) he considers the world situation seri-ous; (3) the committee is unable to make any decisions.

The networks will have interviewed a dozen or so sen-ators from that same hearing. You can wager this senator will make the show. He was brief. He had a "therefore." And he said it with some color.

During a committee hearing some years ago, a House Education Subcommittee was interrogating the Secretary of Education. At issue were severe budget cuts designed by Budget Director David Stockman and offered in the new financial package submitted by President Reagan.

Congressman Peter Peyser, a Democrat from Westchester County in New York, seemed to understand the necessity of putting into a succinct line his critique of the Reagan budget and its architect, Mr. Stockman. To the Secretary of Education, Peyser said: "In many ways, Mr. Secretary, I feel very sorry for you. President Reagan doesn't understand what is involved and David Stockman really doesn't care. He is like a bomber pilot flying high: He can't see the bodies he's destroying."

When the evening news show appeared that day, the editors had a ton of film to consider. Congressman Peyser survived the cut. His three brief sentences captured the color of the hearings.

Don't rely on intuition or inspiration to keep you flying. You may feel confident that you can wing it, but lights and camera can disrupt even the sternest discipline. If you get flustered or ramble, you will be a candidate for an outtake and will be seen only by the film editor and the guy who sweeps up the cutting-room floor.

Think, think, think. Turn over a sentence or two in your mind. How can you phrase your thought to capture public attention? If you have time, jot it down. Read it over several times. If you have a firm grasp of the essentials of what you want to say, your increased confidence will keep you from disarray when the camera points at you.

Television magnifies everything. If you could be given the choice of only one asset to take before the

camera, you would be right to select believability. Even if you don't speak with precision or brevity, if you express your thoughts with complete believability, you are ahead of the game.

A number of corporations are using real people rather than actors in their TV ads: farmers, for example, who extol the virtues of cars or machinery or even household goods. The reason: While the farmer might stumble over his words or speak in rural accents, what comes out is real, not fake. And that is the shining virtue the advertising agency is searching for. Whatever is contrived—in a commercial message or a speech or in a comment by a public figure or businessman—can claim little value.

It is one of the ironies of human nature that those very people—public officials, great corporate captains, civic leaders—who ought to be able to communicate through television are often ill-prepared and, what is worse, even when prepared cannot present a lucid, believable, winning speech or comment.

Keep in mind that these are all public men and women, hardened by the experience of years in the public arena. They could not have risen in the political world without being aware of their mistakes and quickly correcting them. And yet the largest potential weapon in their arsenal, their speaking skills, often remain impervious to criticism by aides and counselors.

Ronald Reagan was an exception. With his long years

of experience before the camera, he learned the craft of communication as few other leaders before him. His voice was rich, innocent of accent or regional tint. His career as an actor endowed him with gifts of delivery unmatched by his contemporaries. And he understood the potential abrasions of television, even as he commanded its assets.

If you will recall the debate between President Carter and Ronald Reagan in the late days of 1980, perhaps you would agree that there was, as in the Kennedy-Nixon debates, one crucial moment when the debate began to slide out of the hands of one candidate and into the other's. It was that moment when, as Carter began to repeat charges against his opponent, Reagan leaned forward, grinned widely, and said, "There you go again." It was such a human response, the sort of laughing accusation a next-door neighbor might make. It blurred Carter's arguments, and completely surprised him. He never really recovered.

Unlike Reagan, Bill Clinton is not a professional actor but he could have been one. Only he and Reagan among latter-day presidents got into their bones and brain the essentials and the ornaments of the television communicator. The bully pulpit that is the White House was theirs to use and they used it to the hilt, with zest and mounting skill.

Corporate leaders, businessmen, education and labor leaders have the opportunity, through closed-circuit television, to speak to their peers, their employees, and their colleagues. They can achieve a rapport with those whom they wish to persuade beyond the capacity of leaders in earlier years when television was not available.

Television defers to the knowledgeable speaker, to the person who appreciates the gaping difference between a large assembly hall and the intimacy of the 21-inch screen. I tried, vainly, to persuade President Johnson to make television his rostrum for explanation, for education, for convincing the public that his decisions were wise and of long-term benefit to the American family.

I proposed a plan for a series of ten-minute telecasts to be aired at 10 P.M. Eastern Standard Time. The ten-minute limit was not casually suggested. It is long enough to say what needs to be said, but not so long as to blot out favorite entertainment programs. (Ten minutes extracted from the regular television schedule is tolerable, but presidential television advisors must never schedule the president at the same time as a popular sporting event. This is blasphemy.) The networks could have easily delayed the start of their regularly scheduled shows for ten minutes without having to cancel entire programs. Hell has a congenial climate by comparison to the wrath of viewers whose favorite sitcom is preempted by a mere president discoursing on the fate of their lives.

My plan was to have the public informed well in advance that the president would not exceed the threshold of tedium. The audience would know that after ten minutes they could settle back to whatever program they were expecting to enjoy.

I suggested that the president review Vietnam in four separate telecasts.

1. Why we are in Vietnam and why it is important to the security of the nation and the families directly affected by the war.
2. How are we doing?
3. Is it possible to reconstruct Vietnam peacefully and are we prepared to do it?
4. Is there the possibility of lasting peace after the fighting has been concluded, and is that a worthy cause to support?

I suggested that the president make similar broadcasts about other difficult problems the nation faced. For instance, the question of pollution and the damage to our environment; the injury to the national economy and health if pollution were allowed to consume all that was clean and fresh in the land. This needed to be explained in simple, understandable language. Issues of crime, urban sprawl, and waste, the evil legacies of inflation, and other hard-to-grasp and even harder-to-solve problems would be suitable for this forum.

The use of television as a rostrum was essential to this kind of leadership—the president as educator-communicator, speaking to the people, explaining, simplifying, pointing out problems, and offering solutions

that would involve the public in their long-range imple-
mentation.

But the president could not invade the TV screen too
often or he might debase his appearances with repetition.
If familiarity indeed breeds contempt, there was a fine line
to be drawn between maintaining mystery and fulfilling
need. The more a leader visits the living rooms of his
constituency, the less exotic is his aura and the less attentive the hospitality.

Moreover, the president must choose his subjects carefully. His crisis speeches—when he has a specific and ur-
gent necessity to communicate with the people about a
clear-cut concern demanding immediate action—must
be set apart from appearances intended to educate the
public.

Impact and receptivity are important elements in the
leader's public report card. Those to whom he speaks,
those he tries to lead, are also those who grade him. But
the requisite without which all is lost is the ability of the
leader to speak reasonably, amiably, and believably, and
if possible, to be inspiring.

I was never able to convince President Johnson of the
wisdom of this educational approach. To this day I don't
know why.

The intelligent use of television not only by public officials but also by leaders in other arenas has to be carefully studied. It is no longer suitable, if it ever was, to
read something on television and expect viewers to be
excited or interested or persuaded.

The first step is to make what you say compact. The maxim applies to a president addressing grave matters of state, a business leader exhorting his sales force, a school superintendent rallying her teachers: Leisurely disquisitions lose their momentum.

Those who are on television for whatever reason should understand the large truth of Occam's Razor. This is a relatively obscure rule known mainly to students of philosophy, but its obscurity in no way diminishes its relevance. William of Occam (or Ockham, as it is sometimes spelled) was a Franciscan monk who lived in England in the fourteenth century. He is not well-known today (fourteenth-century sages don't travel well), but he did originate what came to be known as Occam's Razor, which in essence says, "Entities are not to be multiplied without necessity." To put it another way: Don't do with more what you can do with less.

Every time you make any presentation on television keep Occam's Razor in the forefront of your mind. What can be left out because you have already said it or it is obvious, leave out.

Some of our public officials seem to be learning this lesson. Whatever else may be said about television coverage of the U.S. House of Representatives, I am convinced that the quality of speechmaking in that body is improving in both style and brevity—which only admirers of the turgid and interminable will find regrettable. With the advent of television in the House, even though the members cannot be sure of how many attentive viewers they have, the mere awareness that someone is watching out there is bound to curb the oratorical flourishes.

The second step is to consider the response you want from the viewing audience. If you are trying to win them to your point of view, you must make that viewpoint as attractive as you can. You must build upon a well-reasoned foundation. Cite the problem, sound the alarm where it threatens, and propose a course of action to solve it. You may reproach those who oppose or disagree with you, but you must always consider the feelings of the people you are trying to enlist in your cause.

Third, you must remember that in a large hall a reasonable amount of body movement is perfectly acceptable, sometimes even required. But in the confines of a viewer's living room, the television camera captures you with a more brutal scrutiny than you may like. It is fine to express passion in your cause, but without flailing arms and shaking head. On television, passionate belief is better expressed by a gaze or an emotional inflection of a phrase than by an outthrust fist or jaw.

Fourth, and hardest to learn: To win and hold an audience's attention, you must try to make everything you say interesting. Alas, there is no formula readily available: X units of content plus Y units of emotional appeal times

Z units of persuasiveness equals Audience Interest. You are not dealing with Boyle's Law of Gases where the equations are clean-shaped and final. You can learn only from experience before a camera, mistakes made and never repeated, trial and error.

I am always a bit amused when an actor declares that he never watches himself (or herself) on the screen. I suspect this restraint is born of a press agent's imagination, to let the fans know the actor is a modest person, untainted by ego. Get a bet down that the actor does indeed watch his performance, else how will he know how he performed, to learn from mistakes, to fasten more securely on what he did right?

The fact is that anyone who appears on television would be well advised to try to watch a tape of that experience. You learn by what you see yourself doing. Do you fidget? Do your hands clasp and unclasp as you speak? Where you thought you were expressing certainty, did you actually grimace? Do you blink incessantly? Do your eyes wander as you speak? Does your mouth droop? Or do you have a habit of smiling at the end of each sentence even though you have just predicted Armageddon at two o'clock next Tuesday? Does your voice waver? Do you drop your voice when it ought to rise?

Take careful note of your behavior even when you think the camera is not on you. Recently, an important government official was a guest on a television network press conference. He was apparently ignorant of the significance of the red light on the live camera. When the interviewer was speaking, the official began to scratch himself, unaware that every curl of his wiggling fingers was in full screen view of the audience. It did diminish somewhat his efforts at statesmanship a few seconds later.

Errors noted are usually errors not committed again. We learn by watching what we do, when we do it, and how we do it.

To sum up: Be prepared. Know what you intend to say. If you are using a TelePrompTer in a studio, go over your remarks as often as possible before the red light on the camera goes on. Speak easily; don't try to force anything. Don't get cute or elocutionary. Don't be ponderous. Be yourself. Unease transmits itself to an audience faster than a viral contagion. Study your defects and correct them. Relax. Place friends next to the camera and talk to them; let the camera be simply an eavesdropper.

Why is it that some believe the mere fact of their appearance on television is sufficient to impress and convince their listeners? At the last conference of the Supreme Soviet, after about five minutes of televising the speech of Chairman Brezhnev, the Russian TV camera switched to a studio where a TV announcer actually read the rest of the chairman's two-hour speech. Chairman Brezhnev reappeared on Russian screens for the last two minutes of his speech, possibly to certify that he had made it through without collapsing.

This designated-hitter format, right out of George Orwell's novels, may have been suitable for the USSR, where they could be sure no one would call or write in to protest. But in democratic societies, no one would listen patiently to a reader plodding through a fat text, ignoring everything except the drone of his own voice.

And yet, how often have you watched officials of the government, leaders in labor, business, education, special-interest groups, testifying on television before congressional committees? And how often do these high-powered witnesses—sitting before the microphone, aware that cameras are on them—bury their heads in a thick sheaf of documents and drone on, as they read with fixed gaze every line of every page without so much as a nod to those who are listening?

Many handsomely paid executives, lawyers, professional people, even elected and nonelected government officials who surely know better, obviously believe themselves exempt from the rules of persuasion. There is no attempt to engage the interest of those to whom they are speaking, no attempt to leaven the bulky written pages with any form of human contact—even though their audience is a committee they are trying to persuade to their point of view, not to mention countless others watching in front of TV sets. The congresspeople and senators who are duty-committed to sit through these dreary recitals are earning their public keep during such hearings. Viewers are not so duty-bound. They can turn to other channels.

There are lessons here for business executives who testify before committees of Congress or state legislatures or any other group they must report to or persuade.

The first lesson to be learned before you testify anywhere, before a congressional committee, the city council, or the school board, is: Don't read your presentation in its entirety. Most businessmen or industrial leaders will prepare a long, often dreary, recital of facts and logic, and—to the regret of those who listen—will read the whole text.

The second lesson is: By editing your oral presentation to more sensible limits, you will gain more time to answer your listeners' questions. In the question period you can expand on your oral comments, and offer more detailed explanations of your edited text.

Edit. Prune. Extract everything you wish to emphasize and reassemble those thoughts in your

oral presentation. If you have a fifty-page document you are presenting for the record, you ought to pare it down to no more than three pages. This is essential if you wish to be persuasive. It is far more effective if you don't read your oral statement. But if you absolutely have to, go over it twenty times so that you are speaking directly to the committee at least three quarters of the time and letting your eyes drop to your script no more than one quarter of the time.

———

Whenever I testify before a Committee in the House or the Senate, I zealously keep my oral remarks to five minutes, which is the limit the chairman fastens on witnesses, though some try to plow through that barricade. I also never read my statement. Never. Moreover, I try never to keep any notes on the table in front of me. If you are testifying before Congress on an issue that you know very well, there is no reason why you cannot so prepare yourself that you do not need any text to guide you. The place in front of me is barren, only the microphone between me and my most important audience sitting up there, usually at an oval up-raised dais. I am trying to convey to the Members on the dais that I know my business, that I don't need props or notes to inform me, and that I am going to speak to them directly with no barriers between us. Finally, I try to be entertaining as well as substantive. Members are constantly present at

hearing after hearing, faced with an avalanche of witnesses unacquainted with even a fragment of enticement.
Members of Congress are not gods, but human beings,
who are capable of being bored by a presentation even as
you and I are. Therefore, I try hard (sometimes I don't
succeed) to say what I want to say in as engaging a manner as I possibly can.

CHAPTER SEVEN

Language

*How to Compose Your Speech to
Achieve Your Objective*

Some years ago I attended the Indian Film Festival in
New Delhi. It was a most impressive visit for me. As
the leader of the United States delegation to the festival,
I was obliged to attend several conferences and seminars.
At one of the latter, a well-known Asian film expert, flu-
ent in English, rose to speak about the worldwide infat-
uation with film.

Here is a paragraph from his speech:

> The theory that there exists a Cartesian polar-
> ity between arbitrary aesthetic signs and total re-
> alism necessarily led to quantitative conclusions
> and meaningless oppositions: the proliferation of
> detail as against metaphysical truth, where quality
> cannot be seized, the fluidity of mise-en-scene as
> against meter of montage, the existential tension

of suspense in Hitchcock, as against the tragic release from pity and fear.

I cite this as an example of an attempt to impress an
audience with a combination of words that should never
have been spoken, or written, or even imagined.

What one says is as important as how one says it.
However, while it is possible that a badly drafted speech
may receive renewed life in the throat of an inspired orator, it is also true that a poor speaker can infect a bril-
liantly composed speech with the rickets.

It was reported that in the last few days of his life
Benjamin Disraeli, ill and haggard, sat up in his bed to
correct the proofs of his final speech. "I will not go down
to posterity speaking bad grammar," he said.

All of this is preface to emphasizing the importance of
preparing a speech so that it reads well, has glimpses of
style, is clear in its message, and offers ample opportunity
for the speaker to inform, persuade, convince, and/or entertain.

**The first step in preparing a written speech,
whether you intend to read it verbatim, speak it from
notes, or memorize it, is to know what you want to
accomplish and then to plan carefully how you will
achieve your goal.**

In an article in the *New York Times* on July 4, 2001, Robert D. McFadden suggested that Thomas Jefferson's elegant prose, which exalted the Declaration of Independence, was "something visually poetic, perhaps even musical, a script for a reading performance." Precisely. In the same article Professor Jay Fliegelman of Stanford is quoted (in re Jefferson's prose), "It's a piece of music that has to be played on the human voice." Few of us will be able to emulate Jefferson, but all of us have to be aware of the language with which we frame a speech.

There are three parts to a speech, though they do not necessarily follow in precise order, and they may be repeated within the speech.

> *The first is some humor or wit, some attempt to lighten the more serious aspects of your message—if it is appropriate to do so. If it is not, leave the humor out.*
>
> *The second is to convincingly present the purpose of your speech.*
>
> *The third is to invest your speech with prose that conveys the substance you want your audience to grasp, and to do it as interestingly as you possibly can.*

One helpful suggestion for drafting a speech is to recall the tenets of a great teacher of acting, Charles Jehllinger, who taught for many years at the American

Academy of Dramatic Arts in New York. His pupils included Spencer Tracy, Robert Walker, Rosalind Russell, Katharine Hepburn, and Kirk Douglas. He admonished his students to be ever conscious, as they recited their lines, of thought, theme, and mood. I refer to it as TTM.

Consider this acronym as you prepare what you want to say.

> *What is the* thought *you want to convey?*
> *What is the* theme *of your presentation?*
> *What* mood *do you want to evoke?*

TTM can be a guide for you, as valuable to the most inexperienced speaker as it is to an aspiring actor. While you may not have considered the similarity, it does exist: An actor is performing on a stage to engage an audience, and so are you when you rise to speak. While it is true that the actor is speaking lines written by someone else, and you are probably saying what you have composed yourself, there is a more than casual connection between the actor's objectives and your own.

You don't have to be a professional actor, but you are performing—that is, like the actor, your object is to be believed by those who listen to you, to awake their interest, to gain a rapport with the audience. You may not win an Oscar or a Tony for your efforts, but you do have to be aware that you are "performing" before an audience.

Language

Long ago I was enchanted by the writings of and became a disciple of Descartes. His rules of logic, while applying directly to the solving of almost any problem—financial, political, entrepreneurial, or scientific—can also inform your preparation of a speech. They make a corollary to TTM.

The rules are:

1. Discard everything except that which you know to be true.
2. Break the subject down into as many parts as possible.
3. Start with the parts that are easiest to understand and progress to the hardest.
4. Summarize.

Think for a minute how Descartes can aid you in preparing a speech.

Use that which you know to be true and can certify as such.

Consider what you want to say to the audience and divide it into simple parts. Keep in mind the need to make your audience understand what you are saying. When President Reagan made his economic speech to the nation, he started with simple equations and visual aids that provided a foundation for an examination of the terribly complex issue of inflation.

If you are able to write a speech worth making, by summarizing briefly you can give your thoughts additional impact. You may begin your speech with a summary of what you intend to say and end your speech with a summary of what you have said. But a summary should be little more than a sentence or two.

If I were asked to draft a presidential speech on an economic program to be presented to the people, this is how (using the advice of Descartes) I would begin:

Tonight, my fellow citizens, I present to the American people a plan designed to lift the quality of our economy, so the future of the American family will be safer, healthier, more meaningful, and more prosperous.

This plan that I will present to the Congress will achieve five goals:

1. *It will increase the productivity of American industry.*
2. *It will provide incentive for factories, business, and corporations to increase jobs, with specific emphasis on teenage employment as well as on shrinking the rate of adult unemployment.*
3. *It will halt the spiral of inflation and bring that contagion down to gentler levels.*

4. *It will generate more vigorous American trade abroad.*

5. *It will encourage American business to renovate old equipment, and design and order new equipment.*

Higher productivity, more jobs, increased export trade, modernizing American industry, reducing inflation: That is our program. That is what we are resolved to do. And here is our plan for doing it, a plan that requires the cooperation of each of you listening to me tonight.

Note that the speech immediately breaks down what is to follow under five different headings; it summarizes the task.

The speech would then detail each part of the plan: Why it is being offered, how it will be implemented, what the results will be, and how the individual American family will benefit.

After the details have been itemized, the speech should once more repeat the goals of the plan and summarize what will be done.

With Descartes's guidance, we have shaped a speech that tries to be clear and comprehensible, that attempts to lay out complex problems in doses easy to assimilate, and that frequently summarizes the goals of the plan so that even those who listen with half an ear will grasp the essence of both the plan and the plea.

This is an example of how it is possible to deal with abstruse and speculative matters in language that is both accessible and revealing.

The composition of a speech begins with the objective of the speech. What is your goal? What do you want your audience to feel and think when you have finished?

The essential first step, then, is the careful marking of the objective. The more advance time you spend in defining what you want to achieve, the greater the possibility you will achieve it. Therefore, clear the way for your speech with as precise a design as you can construct.

At the 1980 Democratic National Convention in New York, Senator Edmund Muskie of Maine, himself a former contender for his party's presidential nomination, approached the rostrum to introduce a film depicting the life of the late Hubert Humphrey. I was one of those counseling Senator Muskie on the organization of his remarks.

The senator determined that he wanted to lift the spirits of those present with a brief speech about the personal vibrancy of the former vice president. Appropriately, Muskie aimed at raising the emotional level of the assembly. He wanted the spirit of Humphrey to invade the hall, arousing the delegates as if Humphrey had returned to life with all his talent for the stirring of passionate beliefs in fervent causes.

This is an abridged version of what he said that evening, an example of a speech delivered with its purpose realized. As you read it, watch for the deliberate rhythms of its prose. Long sentences are followed by short ones; explanatory sentences are succeeded by hammer-strong briefer ones. In the very first paragraph there is a natural progression from Humphrey's sterling qualities to the introduction of his name.

Ask yourself how you would improve on the balancing of the cadence, and on the recounting of what Humphrey stood for, what he believed in, and why he was who he was. Each line in this speech was carefully constructed. This is not to say it was ideally constructed or could not be improved, but it was not put together casually. Any speech that aspires to be good should be attended to with care, given thought and time, and not hobbled by uneven concentration or inattention to detail.

> *My Fellow Citizens:*
>
> *I come before you tonight to speak of love and laughter, of wisdom and warmth, of duty and honor. I come before you to measure a terrible loss and to remind you of a joyous legacy. I come to speak of Hubert Humphrey.*
>
> *Almost thirty-two years ago to this very hour, in another Democratic convention in Philadelphia, this thirty-seven-year-old mayor of Minneapolis, and a candidate for the United States*

Senate, rose to his feet and with a single speech electrified the entire nation. The sound of his voice became the herald and the inspiration of both a party and a country. He spoke the words that lit up a dark corner of the American soul.

This hall tonight is crowded with those who knew Hubert so very well. Can we not see and hear him now, vibrating with ideas, spilling over with the enthusiasm that would have broken the shield of the grumpiest among us?

Behind the infectious Humphrey grin existed a man always in full command of the resources of the most fertile political mind any one of us has ever encountered. No combination of peril and embarrassment would perplex him. No danger could daunt him.

He was an intellectual who spoke the language of the village square. He endured defeat because he believed that defeat was never final and setbacks only momentary. He kept his eye on the distant objective and not the one nearest him.

He was that most peculiar of all public men. He never hated. He never swore vengeance. Sometimes he was the bearer of unrecognized truth. But eventually, what he declared to be right soon claimed the allegiance of those who saw only dimly what he saw so clearly.

It is shameful that he never became president.

Language

It is an act of national omission that time will never expunge.

There are two methods to creating a speech. You may determine which method is more congenial to you.

FIRST METHOD

Sketch out on paper fairly detailed notes on what you want to convey, the points you want to emphasize, and the impression you want to make on your audience. This is essential. Unless you have a clear idea of what you want to say, it is doubtful you will say anything worth remembering.

Then dictate your speech into a tape recorder or to a secretary. By this method, you are speaking to an audience much as you talk conversationally. (Some people don't find dictating quite suitable to them. If you are one of them, then see the second method, below.)

In your first dictated draft, don't bother to give what you are saying a finished tone. Keep talking. When you are done, have that draft typed. Now, go over it carefully. Extract any repetitions you find. Smooth the rough edges so that the sentences parse, and make sure no explanation is extraneous to your theme. Check over any statistics you use to ensure their accuracy.

With your first draft in hand, speak again into the tape recorder. If there is anything in the speech that gives you problems, revise as you go; that is, stop the tape recorder and make any changes you find necessary. Go through the entire speech adding whatever persuasive elements are required to gain and hold the attention of your audience.

You will now be ready to decide whether to give your speech from your finished text or to use notes. Go with whichever form makes you feel more comfortable. Keep in mind that as a rule a speech is more effective when delivered from notes than when read from a prepared text. But if you are tense with anxiety and the feeling that you are walking a tightrope without a safety net, you will probably detract less from the quality of your presentation if you opt for the prepared text.

Sir Winston Churchill usually prepared his speeches and books by this method. He adapted his singular abilities to the service of the spoken word, and through his rare chemistry of wit and literacy and his classic style of prose construction, many a sentence emerged like a pearl from an oyster shell, finely polished, shining, and symmetrical. Writing many years later about how his poor schoolwork at Harrow had resulted in enforced repetition of classes, including grammar and composition, he said, "I got into my bones the structure of the simple English sentence, which is a noble thing indeed."

The youthful Churchill was, as many of us are, a slow and awkward learner. In his early parliamentary career he was very good at assembling a set speech, carefully prepared in the classic tradition, but he was then something less than an eloquent speaker. Lord Balfour (nephew of a previous prime minister and later the crown's first minister himself) once said of Churchill's early speaking style: "He carried heavy but not very mobile guns."

Churchill also had great skill in editing his own material. He required his publishers to set type for every book, and then would rewrite extensively.

But there are few Churchills in a generation. We lesser mortals must be content with a literacy less comprehensive and an eloquence less spellbinding.

On June 20, 1940, the House of Commons went into secret session to hear the new British prime minister. Under the rules of the Commons, no recording of such speeches is ever made. There is no accurate historical accounting of what is spoken by the members. A pity—but then, the Commons has existed for more than seven hundred years, sufficient to attest to the durability of the English system without the need for sage counsel from outsiders like me.

Winston Churchill, in all his other appearances in secret sessions during the war, carefully prepared his speeches, wrote them out, and preserved them for his own personal record. But on this June 20, he did not.

What he did do was think about his remarks with the systematic precision he employed, with inveterate success, over the years of his stewardship, and put to paper a series of notes from which he drew his final speech.

Here are the notes (which I have edited for brevity's sake) that Churchill used in that secret-session speech. In the British Archives one may see, written in Churchill's own hand, the scratchy annotations with which he embellished his speech shortly before he rose to deliver it.

Secret Session. House of Commons.

My reliance on it as an instrument for waging war.

More active and direct part for its Members L.D.V.

All this in accordance with past history. This S.S. a model of discretion.

My view always Govt. strengthened by S.S.

Agree with idea S.S. shd be quite a normal part of our procedure, not associated with any crisis.

Relief to be able to talk without enemy reading.

Quite ready to have other S.S.s, especially on precise subjects.

But I hope not press Ministers engaged in conduct of war too hard.

Mood of the House. Cool and robust.

Speeches most informative. Difficult to betray any secrets disclosed today.

Politicians and Generals,

In last war and this.

Not put too much on the politicians: even they may err.

Goering. How do you class him? He was an airman turned politician.

I like him better as an airman. Not very much anyway.

This supreme battle depends upon the courage of the ordinary man and woman.

Fate of Northern Armies sealed when the G. armoured Divisions curled round their whole communication. Abbeville, Boulogne, Calais.

Not 2 days' food. Only ammunition one battle.

Quite impossible with Air attack on ports. One in three supply ships sunk.

Situation looked terrible, especially when Belgium gave in.

Give all credit to all three Forces.

Army fought its way back; Navy showed its wonderful reserve power; Air Force rendered naval work possible.

B.E.F. a fine Army. Only 10 Divisions.

That will play its part; but essence of defence of Britain is to attack the landed enemy at once, leap at his throat and keep the grip until the life is out of him.

We have a powerful Army growing in strength and equipment every day.

Many very fine Divisions.

Vigilant coast watch. Strong defence of ports and inlets.

If Hitler fails to invade or destroy Britain he has lost the war.

If enemy coastline extends from Arctic to Mediterranean and we retain sea power and a growing air power it is evident that Hitler, master of a starving, agonized and surging Europe, will have his dangers as well as we.

Attitude of United States. Nothing will stir them like fighting in England.

The heroic struggle of Britain best chance of bringing them in.

A tribute to Roosevelt.

All depends upon our resolute bearing and holding out until Election issues are settled there.

If we can do so, I cannot doubt a whole English-speaking world will be in line together and with the Oceans and with the Air and all the Continents except Europe (RUSSIA).

Lastly, say a word about ourselves.

How the new Govt. was formed.

Tell the story Chamberlain's actions.

Imperative there should be loyalty, union among men who have joined hands.

Otherwise no means of standing the shocks and strains which are coming.

Language

*I have a right to defend loyalty to the admin-
istration and feel we have only one enemy to face,
the foul foe who threatens our freedom and our
life, and bars the upward march of man.*

See the evidence: "Fate of Northern Armies sealed
when the G. armoured Divisions curled round their whole
communication."

See again the use of a quotable phrase written in the
notes: "leap at his throat, and keep the grip until the life
is out of him." And again: "it is evident that Hitler, master of a starving, agonized and surging Europe."

These notations verify that Churchill never abandoned
his insightful use of the baroque clause, the identifying
imprint of Churchillian prose, which vexes his literary
critics.

One more important element: His final paragraph was
written out in full, so that he would not have to forage
for the right words to conclude his presentation to the
Commons.

These notes provided Churchill with the framework
for his message. He had years of practice and confidence
in his ability to clothe the brief phrases of his notes in
oratorical velvet, weaving each note with the one before
and the one after in a seamless whole.

Obviously, none of us will be able to duplicate this
unique talent. But what can be learned is the technique
of preparation. How successful the results are depends on

the time and energy one is ready to invest. It is fair to state that any speech is improved by the diligence of the writer's preparatory work.

The speech you make need not grapple with the profound issues of life and death, the survival of a nation and a civilization, as Churchill's did. But when you report on a corporate plan to your fellow employees or propose a project to your civic organization, the labor required remains the same. It is simply a matter of giving enough thought to what you are going to say, deciding how you will develop your message, and then dictating into a tape recorder.

Finally, when the finished text is done, it is a good idea to recite it once more into the tape recorder, this time for intonation, for inflection, for emphasis given to matters of importance, and for timing.

Listen to the tape over and over again. Make notes on your text where you believe an upbeat tone is required or where you think you should lower your voice to draw greater attention, by contrast, to what may follow.

SECOND METHOD

In this method, you write out your speech in advance. In long hand or on a computer, you build your speech as you would a letter, an essay, or a memorandum to a friend whose support is necessary to your cause.

I find this method personally more satisfying because I like to see the words form in front of me. I would much rather write my speeches on a computer than dictate them. I am attracted to the serried march of the words as I compose my text. The speech becomes more familiar because I have watched it grow before my eyes.

Some years ago I was selected to present to John D. Rockefeller III the prestigious Jefferson Award of the American Institute of Public Service. I deliberated for a good many hours over the theme of that presentation. My aim was to encapsulate, in less than five minutes, the life of Mr. Rockefeller, and to do so in a fashion calculated to enlighten the audience not only about his work, with which all were familiar, but more notably about the form and force of his character.

My audience would be largely Washingtonian, men and women experienced in politics, literate, and informed about current affairs. They would be people who either knew Rockefeller personally or at least were knowledge-able about his life's work. Therefore I wanted to give some emotional weight to what I said, above and beyond relating the specifics of his actions.

I determined that my theme would be the Rockefeller family and that family's persistent acceptance of their ob-ligation to a country that had provided them with the means to enormous wealth.

I began to write, bending every word to the purpose of my theme. I found the first draft unsatisfying. It was too long and it lacked continuity. So I wrote out a second draft and a third. Then I revised the third draft, excising some lines that did not fit and modifying those that needed some small lift.

Finally, I finished the last draft and turned on my tape recorder. I read the speech and then listened carefully to what I had said. I found some phrases awkward on the tongue, such as "commitments flimsily kept." The word-flimsy, though ideally descriptive for my purpose, works better in print than spoken aloud. I simply could not say "flimsily kept" without slurring. I blotted it out and inserted "not redeemed." It served my meaning, if not the symmetry, just as well—and I could say it without faltering.

I also had a phrase, "weep real tears," which frankly I liked, but my tongue skidded across the *p* of "weep" and collided with the *r* of "real." I struck out "real tears" and went with "weep" alone. This was not as good a piece of imagery as I had intended, but I felt calmer about saying *weep* than running the risk of skittering across the entire phrase.

I had timed the presentation at three minutes, fifteen seconds. Allowing for any digression I might make at the last minute or any extemporizing I would do, I felt I could handle this presentation within my absolute limit of three minutes forty-five seconds.

This is what I said:

> *My old boss President Johnson was apt to use the homely language of Texas ranch-country genetics when he wanted to describe the achievements of a great family. He used to say warmly*

about the Rockefeller family: [a slight pause] "By god, there is <u>something</u> in the stud."

The Rockefeller family has devoted itself to lifting the <u>excellence</u> and the <u>quality of life</u> in this nation, and around the world. There is a fragile nobility to <u>that</u> kind of goal. It can be so easily shattered by commitments <u>not</u> redeemed [slight pause] or pledges <u>casually</u> neglected. Mr. Rockefeller and his family have achieved their objectives in the unaltered conduct of their lives. Theirs has been a straight clean line through <u>three</u> generations [pause slightly] and is alive and moving—in a <u>fourth</u>.

We live in what Shakespeare might have called "a scrambling and unquiet time." It is comforting to a good many people that even so, there are some qualities that are proof against the <u>erosion of excellence</u>.

The worth of Mr. Rockefeller can be measured only if you believe in ancient values, [pause] in the meaning of <u>justice</u> and <u>compassion</u>, [pause] if you can <u>weep</u> at the misery of those who are pressed against the wall because of the meanness of chance over which <u>so few of us</u> have any real control.

No Republic can <u>long</u> survive unless there exists in the community a replenishing supply <u>each</u> generation of honorable men and women who

worry <u>not at all</u> about social fads or political fash-
ions. They live by <u>sterner codes</u>. They are unre-
lieved by moral shortcuts. Mr. Rockefeller and his
family belong to <u>this band of caring citizens.</u>

Mr. Rockefeller has won this award <u>not only</u>
because of his long and rewarded efforts in pop-
ulation control but because he has been involved
in <u>educating</u> the nation in a number of unpopular
issues. As chairman of the Rockefeller Founda-
tion, he has been a <u>quiet</u> and unobtrusive man.
But every day of his life he has been involved in
<u>helping others</u> live a better life.

Elbridge Gerry, one of the founding fathers,
probably valued the Rockefeller family goal ac-
curately when he said in the birth year of the Re-
public: "The whole business of life [slight pause]
is to <u>serve</u> your country."

It is the <u>best</u> one-line description of Mr.
Rockefeller that I know.

Woodrow Wilson had a gift for the phrase that lingers
in the mind. Often his speeches were lit with special,
memorable passages, such as "the fundamental rights of
humanity," "watchful waiting," "peace without victory."
These pithy two- and three-word phrases that people can
store up in memory are the essence of vivid indelible
speechmaking.

President Wilson was always conscious of the power
of the human voice to plead, amuse, inspire, terrify,

soothe, and eventually persuade. He used the spoken word as often as he could, not wishing to rely on the printed message alone. It was he who revived a tradition begun by George Washington and John Adams, and later set aside by Thomas Jefferson (who, though a gifted writer, was not eloquent or even modestly inspiring in speech), to present to the Congress in person the presidential State of the Union message.

To catch the minds of your listeners and force them to remember what you have said is the second highest goal to which a speaker can aspire. The first is to persuade them.

Former Minnesota Senator Eugene McCarthy once said of Hubert Humphrey: "Humphrey's detractors accuse him of talking too much. That is unfair. His fault is that when he says things, he says them in a way that people remember. It's dangerous for a national candidate to say things people remember!"

In Franklin Roosevelt's speech on Washington's birthday in 1942, the old master was in high form as he catalogued grim facts about the war in the jaunty, stylish manner he made so famous. As you read, you can almost hear the patrician accents of his voice:

> From Berlin, Rome and Tokyo we have been described as a nation of weaklings—playboys— who would hire British soldiers or Russian soldiers or Chinese soldiers to do our fighting for us.
>
> Let them repeat that now!

Let them tell that to General MacArthur and his men.

Let them tell that to the sailors who today are hitting hard in the waters of the Pacific.

Let them tell that to the boys in the Flying Fortresses.

Let them tell that to the Marines.

This was a typical FDR speech, delivered with high good humor—and a mailed fist.

It is true that quotable, freshly minted phrases have a way of winning audiences, but if you are a beginner, or still wrestling with the quirks of speaking before groups, keep what you say as simple as you can.

As you go about composing what you choose to say, keep some simple pointers in mind:

1. Draw up an outline, however brief, of what you want to get across, including some of the specific points you want to make.

2. Try not to introduce too many elements into your speech. That is, don't spread your gospel too thin,

with too many points to make and remember. If you are delivering a report to your civic group on a number of projects, that is quite all right. But if you are giving the audience something more than a list of plans and their implementations, try to eliminate all but one or two key points.

3. Don't hesitate to seek out people you respect for ideas, or even phrases you might use. Don't let pride or any other inconvenient scruple keep you from asking others for their judgment.

4. As you construct your speech, never forget that this is not an exercise in personal indulgence; you are striving to make contact with your audience. Don't hesitate to throw out anything that is excess baggage. (I confess this is my largest sin in speaking, for I find the counsel I give you now the most difficult to follow myself.)

   Metaphors, as I can painfully recall, are apt to do a speaker in unless they are carefully crafted. William Safire, the *New York Times* columnist, recounted a story about Senator Everett Dirksen, Republican leader during the LBJ presidency, and his brave attempts to use the metaphor with precision. Safire reported that Senator Dirksen rose in the Senate to say "At last we have a firm hand on the rudder of the ship of state." Granting that this phrase does not break new ground in the field of persuasion, Safire explained: "Dirksen enlisted the power of a nautical metaphor even though his speech writer was chagrined later to learn that the man with the hand on the rudder would be drowning and nobody would be minding the tiller."

5. Hark back to the brief passage from FDR's Washington's birthday speech. Note the short, slingshot sentences. They are spare, without elaborate ornamentation. They are like the hammer that pounds the nail that seals the cask. They are drivingly effective in this short passage, but an entire speech made up of such sentences would be staccato. If you compose a long sentence, try to follow it with a shorter one. There is a reason for this recommendation besides rhythmic balance. Unless you are trained in breathing, if you string out too many long sentences you are apt to find yourself gulping in air to refuel your lungs, which is a touch clumsy.

6. Use words that are readily understandable, as clear in meaning as you can make them. Seek out every now and then a saucier word than the usual one, to give what you say a brighter tinge. But don't move too quickly in this area; give yourself some practice time, testing gradually your ability to add the spice

of a new expression to something that is plainly true.

7. Always try to summarize what you have said. Implant in your audience a closing reminder of what it is that you would impress upon their memories.

CHAPTER EIGHT

Grading Presidential
Speaking Styles

The president is the living exemplar of the unique tis-
sue that connects winning the confidence and affection of the people to the ability to embrace American
voters through the medium of television. In short, if
you're president and you want to achieve high favorable
ratings from the voters, you had best be able to speak to
them so that they will like you and want to watch you
and listen to you. Indeed, if you want to be elected president and sustain the favor of a majority of the citizenry,
you had better realize that television is the prime forum
for such a hoped-for triumph.

There's a lesson here that every president has to understand with great clarity. It is this: in presidential cam-
paigns some 98 percent or more of the American people
will never see the presidential candidate in person; they
will only see him or her on their television set. Out of
that screen in their home will come all they will know
about the candidate. How he or she looks and speaks,

what they say and most of all the way they say it will shape and form public opinion. Like it or not, presidents are "actors." They are performers on stage. When they speak, they, like actors, are trying to persuade an audience to believe them and like them.

What a good many intellectual savants and political critics fail to truly absorb as a fundamental fact is that in a presidential election the vast majority of people in this land vote viscerally, *not* intellectually. We vote romantically, not rationally, with our heart and not our head. So it is that we connect emotionally—or not—to presidential candidates when we meet them for the first time when they come into our homes via the TV screen. We form impressions. The impressions guided by these visual visits are quickly conveyed to our emotions, which in turn decide how we vote.

That's why the ability (or the inability) of the presidential candidate to win us over depends almost entirely on how he or she speaks to us via television. This is not to say that issues are unimportant. Not at all. The issues of war and peace or an economic meltdown count mightily. But after you subtract from the total vote those who are rigidly manacled to combustible issues like abortion or gun control or whatever, the remainder of the population is the majority that will elect the president. The other issues in any presidential election are usually so complicated, squirming with complexities, so resistant to clear solutions that few of us are capable of deciphering the numbers and the ambiguities that infect political rhetoric. We have all heard candidates for president preach budget arithmetic to us, as well as expound on the murkily formed sinews of Social Security and Medicare, or whether missile shields work or don't work—and the list goes on. Honestly, can any voter truly know the differences, and if any one of us does, how do we know who's right? The man or woman who is elected president is the one who invades the heart of the voter, whose self-presentation entices voters. It is a visceral entwining, and more often than not, that rapport is gained almost entirely through the speaking ability of the president.

Go through the list of presidents beginning with the World War II era and you will grasp the connection between voter favor and disfavor, the persuasion skills of the victorious candidate, and the lack of them in the loser. Here, then, is my "Report Card" showing how I grade presidents from FDR to George W. Bush on their ability to speak to the people they have by solemn oath sworn to serve.

FRANKLIN ROOSEVELT: Grade A+. The greatest of all American presidents in speaking ability. If there had been television in his time he could have been elected for life, so all-embracing was his electrifying effect on those who heard him. Newsreels that captured him on film confirm to this day his magical gifts of communication. His elegantly timbered musical voice was the most effective political weapon ever deployed in this nation. With his handsome patrician appearance, FDR looked like a president or how we think a president should look, sound, and act. He knew what powerful effect the sound of his voice had and he used that skill with devoted singularity.

Roosevelt and Winston Churchill, by some divine alchemy, occupied the world stage at the same time. It was their speeches on radio, their premeditated attention to the assembly of words, rhythm, clarity, and eloquence that for a long time were the sole defense (along with brave but pitifully few pilots in the RAF) of an almost collapsing free world. Young people who have no knowledge of FDR ought to listen to some of his speeches and watch some of those newsreels. Prepare yourself to be totally beguiled.

HARRY S TRUMAN: Grade C−. He was better in retrospect than he was in office. His voice was flinty, nasal, disinviting. His gestures were choppy, resembling nothing so much as the metronome-like endless clanking of the metal arms of an old oil well, up and down, up and down to no visible useful purpose. His vocal persuasions were banal, barren of enticement. In his term of office, Truman made brave decisions that, in retrospect, have earned historians' praise. We forget, in view of Truman's latter-day status as one of the highest ranked presidents, that when he left office his favorable ratings were in the low thirties.

Why? He never connected with the public as a leader must do. It took years for political observers to know that the great decisions he made turned out to be right. By that time, Truman was in the last years of his life in Independence, Kansas.

DWIGHT EISENHOWER: Grade B. Ike was not a first-rate speaker, but when he spoke his words marched out borne on the still-alive imagery of a triumphant military commander whose battlefield victories salvaged the future of the free world. In brief, you believed in him because you thought you ought to. Ike fought a losing war with syntax. He never felt comfortable in the collective synergy of voice and dramatic sense. He had no gift for it. His public voice was unremarkable, garmented in flat prairie accents, with no effort to be enticing to audiences. Those who were close to him maintained that in small groups he commanded interest as he commanded his troops, with authority offered with a genial smile and an unyielding resolve. He remained in office and was reelected because the citizens of this country felt comforted having a victorious war leader as their chief executive officer.

JOHN F. KENNEDY: Grade A. JFK was the first TV president. He overcame TV's subtle, serrated challenges with supreme confidence. He understood perfectly the political worth of public charm as a weapon of persuasion. It didn't come to him early. He worked at it. I heard him shortly after he entered the Senate in 1953 in a speech he made in New York at some long-ago forgotten event. His performance was undistinguished. In the next several years he must have been tutored by the best, for when he ran for president in 1960, he was at the top of his TV game.

Kennedy radiated a cool urbanity which became his signature. The famous Kennedy rhythms infatuated TV viewers, the lift and fall of phrases, pitched exquisitely, delivered skillfully. Each public performance was imbued with a self-deprecatory wit and delivered with an easy grace. He mastered the medium.

LYNDON B. JOHNSON: Grade C+. In a room with an audience of some two dozen or so, he was irresistible, unstoppable. His overpowering physical presence was both intimidating and commanding. He devoured all the facts of every issue and was invulnerable to factual re-buttal. His galvanic energy and his relentless pursuit of his convictions could neither be stayed nor swayed by human impediments. But early in his presidency he deter-mined he would substitute his singular persuasive force for a "grandfatherly calm" that he perceived to be "pres-idential." Alas, in his public appearances on TV Johnson came off as boring instead of the exciting leader he surely was in small gatherings.

TV is a harsh arbiter. It exposes someone who is trying to be what he isn't as he tries to hide from the public what he truly is, which in LBJ's case was a political figure of endless fascination and emotional attraction, passionately demanding that America change for the better, particularly for those pressed against the wall because of circumstances over which they had no control. Several times Johnson rose to the occasion and the fires that burned in his belly enthralled his audience. He was at his best at Howard University in 1965 when he lofted the concept of affirmative action, at the University of Michigan in 1964 when he unveiled the Great Society. But it was in the summer of 1965 when, in a speech to the joint session of the Congress, he electrified the nation and brought the entire assembly of the Congress to their feet with his rousing "And we shall overcome." Alas, Johnson mostly offered studied restraint on TV instead of fully revealing the awesome engine of the man that he was. In unharnessed action he was the single most formidable public leader I have ever known or ever will know. LBJ renounced re-nomination and was dead four years later.

RICHARD M. NIXON: Grade D. Of all the modern-day TV presidents, Nixon was the least believable to the public. He was in public appearances a plastic man. On TV his arms jerked about in what appeared to be a constant controversy with the rest of his body; indeed his limbs and his frame were in a perpetual state of enmity. Nixon exuded an air of condescension toward his audience, whether in his famous Checkers speech or his latter-day exhortation, "I am not a crook." It is a bit astonishing to me that Nixon was able to be electorally successful in a career when his speaking equipment was so inadequate. But Nixon was fortunate in his timing: In 1968 he won by less than half of 1 percent, even though Hubert Humphrey came off a devastatingly violent Chicago convention. In 1972, George McGovern, in person a dear, good man, was so out of the political mainstream of America, he offered at best only token opposition.

Nixon was a strange duck, no doubt about it. On the speaking platform he was always suspect. Beads of perspiration populated his forehead, even though the temperature in the room approached Arctic levels. Nixon's smile would appear to light on his lips for a nanosecond and then dart away like a frightened minnow in disagreeable waters. He was incapable of looking relaxed. When he spoke, like a ghost at a seance, he gave off an aura of darkness. The forced smile, the cracking of a stern demeanor, and then the quick reassembly of the shattered parts, the ponderous homily, the awkward turns as he grazed the edges of travesty: these were the unconnected parts of this Lego man.

He *was* gifted with a striking intelligence, as well as a menacing attention to ambition, naked, sharp, and unending. He was never able to introduce himself to what most people would describe as an understanding of the human condition. He held in contempt those who opposed him. He paraded the virtues of the leader uninfected by false faces, but he was, in fact and in life, duplicitous. Nixon's television defects ought to be studied by any serious student of public presentations. Charles de Gaulle may have unknowingly pinpointed one of Nixon's problems when he wrote of "the number of pretensions in which the statesman has to indulge ... the devious methods demanded by the art of government."

GERALD FORD: Grade C−. Along with George H. W. Bush, he was the most decent and sincere of modern-day presidents. It is such a loss that this good man was never able to command the language and exhibit the cadences that mark a modestly capable speaker. I found him immensely alert and knowledgeable in private conversation, able to offer his views in sensible and persuasive fashion. Which was why I was continually surprised when on TV he seemed incapable of speaking a complete thought without groping and searching. He spoke so slowly, as if he were encountering some words for the first time and was suspicious of their entry into his vocabulary. In all his years of public service Ford seldom reached a level of adequacy in public appearances and debates that any national leader in order to lead must achieve. One exception was his "the national nightmare is over" speech delivered shortly after he was sworn in as president. It came straight from his heart, and relieved the anxieties of the American people at precisely the right time.

I always yearned to spend some private time with Ford

to offer him some modest counsel. I wanted him to do better because his integrity and his devotion to his country inhabited his every thought.

JIMMY CARTER: Grade C−. He came into office on a wave of Watergate revulsion. With all his simple and sometimes winsome charm, masterly in his command of facts and detail, he had a singsong delivery and a curious and off-putting way of popping his eyelids at the end of a sentence. In a close-up this took on the aspect of a tic. After a while viewers came to wait for the climax of a thought, and sure enough the eyes popped. I often wondered why President Carter never studied tapes of his TV appearances to correct this distracting mannerism. This is partly why he was unable to grab an audience and enchant them.

It wasn't merely the southern cadences that did him in. It was the lack of empathy with viewers, fed by his deeply grounded vision that he was doing the Lord's work, which enclosed him in a serene but rigid web of righteousness. The clear implication was that those who opposed him were barred from that divine connection.

Carter was much more effective in small groups than with TV appearances. In public he manufactured boredom where none originally existed. There was in almost every TV speech a noticeable exile of excitement. He made eyes glaze over and ears aggressively resistant to whatever he said. He did not win another term in office. Yet in his years out of office, Jimmy Carter became, to most Americans, the exemplar of how an ex-president ought to conduct himself.

RONALD REAGAN: Grade A. Whatever anyone can say about actors as presidents, Ronald Reagan overwhelmed their negative indictments. He knew how to hit his mark and say his lines. In his time he was without question the finest example of how a leader could win over TV audiences with graceful tones and gestures that meshed invisibly with comforting sounds of "the falling of the clauses." There was an ease about him that invariably got into the entrails of those who watched him and made them feel comfortable and safe.

Those political cynics, who roused themselves into frenzy over this Hollywood actor-intruder, never understood, as Reagan did, that all that counts in the political cockpit is to win the favor and the confidence of voters through your connection with them. You are then invulnerable to the sniping and the carping of the critics. If ever the high worth of speaking well was doubted, Reagan quashed the doubters.

In his first national address as president, Reagan spoke about the economy. Listening to a speech about the economy, replete with fiscal arithmetic and abstruse jargon, is usually the best cure for sleeplessness. Lyndon Johnson once remarked, not without truth, that a president making a speech about economics, "was like a man peeing down his leg. It made him feel warm, but no one else knew what the hell he was doing."

Here are Reagan's first few sentences in that economics speech:

> I am speaking to you tonight to give you a report on the state of our national economy.
>
> I regret to say we are in the worst economic mess since the Great Depression. A few days ago I was presented with a report I had asked for, an audit of the economy. I didn't like it. But we have to face the truth and then go to work to turn things around. And make no mistake, we will turn things around. I'm not going to subject you to a jumble of charts, figures, and economic jargon of that audit, but rather try to explain where we are, how we got there, and how we can get back.

He went on from there, briefly, to outline simply what the issue was all about. The use of the word *mess* was apt and understandable to all who listened. No attempt to be eloquent, but merely to be clear. No attempt to be an orator, but only to be lucid and understood. And to say it all in a firm voice, musically formed. I would surmise that Reagan wrote most of that speech himself using words and spacing he felt comfortable with.

Yet the words on paper give little hint of how they

sounded as they leaped from his lips, roundly measured, attended by a smile and a trademark tug of the head. All those years of acting, all the countless speeches he made as an ambassador for his GE television show, sharpened in Ronald Reagan a unique ability to communicate.

GEORGE H. W. BUSH: Grade C. President Bush is but another confirmation that decency of purpose, a genetically inspired love of country and duty, an intellect of high quality, and a war record of undisputed heroism are not enough to win the favor of voters. In the interest of full disclosure, I must mention that the elder President Bush was, next to LBJ, the president for whom I have the most affection and respect.

For reasons unexplained, Bush never learned nor used the indispensable assets that come from first-rate public speaking. When the nation is storm-driven, when there is anxiety or doubt in the land, the leader who will survive is one who can soothe the fevered public brow. The only way to do that is to lift the nation's spirit with personal visits on TV, asking the people to follow you to the mountaintop and arousing them to join in the journey.

Bush had all the equipment to be a great president (historians may so classify him, for as time passes, he will inevitably reach a higher historical standing). He was amply supplied with intellect, principles funded by an unvarying morality, and an understanding of the murky channel ways which compromise the political landscape. Of all the U.S. presidents in the last fifty years of the twentieth century he was, in my judgment, the most knowledgeable about foreign policy. The great omission in his tenure was his failure to use TV as a bully pulpit. He never illuminated public passion for that which he counted to be of high import to the nation. His greatest achievement came in Desert Storm, when he personally enlisted several dozen nations to join in the crusade to deter Saddam Hussein from plundering the Middle East. It was his personal persuasion that not only formed the multination force, but through nerve-wracking times, held it together, a politically Herculean task. This was leadership at its most exalted level, but it was seldom exhibited on TV. I sorrowed because Bush is a man of inexpressibly high honor and intellect. Alas, he did not win another term in office.

BILL CLINTON: Grade A. In spite of all the criticisms one could hurl at Clinton, in spite of his inability to put a disciplined harness on his appetites, in spite of a catalog of constant public battles with the truth that he invariably lost, in spite of weakening the mystique of the Oval Office, culminating in a final week of grotesque misjudgment—to put the best face on it—Clinton remained oddly, amazingly, in touch with most Americans. Why? Because Bill Clinton early on recognized that persistent charm, exhibited in public performances, along with a shrewd assessment of the indispensable value of TV in getting his arms around voters, would be his barricade against all antagonists, inside his party as well as outside.

Clinton was the greatest presidential mourner I have ever seen. Like so many other Americans, I was continually hypnotized when I watched him visit areas hit by tragedy. His eyes grew moist. He hugged and embraced individuals who were collapsing in personal grief. When he would say "I feel your pain," he made that cliché come alive.

Clinton and Ronald Reagan, as different in mood, motive, and conduct as any two men could possibly be, triumphantly conquered the brittle, brutish, knife-edged world of political television. They won their battles on the small and not-so-small screens inhabiting American homes. They knew, understood, and used their speaking skills to win public popularity. But each to different conclusions, and by different personal methods and moral reference.

Moreover, Clinton learned from the speaking blunders he committed. Few of us now remember his introduction of the Democratic Party nominee for president, Michael Dukakis, at the Democratic convention in 1988. Clinton, later the absolute master of the TV screen, forgot the elementary lesson of political introductions: Be engaging but most of all, be brief. He went on, and on, and on, interminably, leaping over one climax and then another, and then another, while the audience fretted in frustration at this speech without end. Finally, Clinton said, "and in conclusion," at which time the entire hall rose to its feet in frenzied gratitude. I daresay no one who watched the proceedings on television would have bet a counterfeit dollar bill that Clinton would be able to survive such a horrendous pratfall, and go on to win the nomination himself four years later.

This was the first sighting of Clinton's Lazarus-like ability to rise from the political dead through the deployment of his television charm. It was not the last of his Houdini-escapes, not by any means, due primarily to his nonpareil TV performances. He never needed a script to guide him, though when he used written texts, he used them as casual aids, never as a life net. If the text had exploded in his hands, he would have doubtless pressed on without hesitation. He knew the asset value of his physical presence. And he deployed with unerring ease a relaxed, comforting manner, a keen sense of eye contact, an occasional "biting of the lip" to confirm his sincerity, all of which worked on viewers. This is mighty hard to learn. I surmise Clinton had it all when he sprang from his mother's womb.

GEORGE W. BUSH: Grade B+. What he brings to the TV table is a genuine warmth of personality. Bush is a "quick learner." He has persistently lifted the level of his public presentations since his presence in office as governor of Texas. I heard him speak in those early gubernatorial days and his improvement at the rostrum is palpable. He has developed a growing skill in "eye contact," that is, not burying himself in a text. He is more confident in using the pause to mounting dramatic effect as well as in delivering humor. It is the ability to grow and learn and the willingness to practice that is the seedbed from which springs a first-class public political TV performer.

On September 20, 2001, nine days after the terrorist attack on America, President Bush spoke to the American people, whose nerve-edges were raw and abused. This nation had just been shattered by a vile intrusion of such uncomprehending lunacy and callousness, it was beyond human belief. President Bush did something that every political leader must do if he is to lay claim to greatness: when the dagger is at the nation's belly, the leader must rise to confront the challenge with such confidence and resolve that the people are comforted, inspired, and attached to his urgings. Bush hit all the right notes. He spoke with firmness. The words were clothed in eloquence. Clarity invested every paragraph. In brief, the speech was an astounding triumph.

If he continues to improve, when George W. Bush's term is done, he will be gauged to be a very effective speaker on television. Bush understands that the soil in which his public favor will take root and blossom will be the television screen.

A Modest Epilogue

WHAT YOU HAVE just finished reading is not the end-all of learning to speak. But it is a beginning.

If you have now resolved that you want to speak with more authority, with more believability, and with more confidence, go back over this book and make notes about its key points.

The first essential word to remember is *think*. Think about what you want to say. Think about the audience you will address. Use TTM—thought, theme, and mood—as your guide. Recall Descartes and his rules of discourse.

Think about brevity and the need to be concise.

Think about how you will phrase what you want to say.

Think about how you are going to be as professional as possible. Don't expect to be the "great orator." Be satisfied with knowing you have done better than you thought you could, but always be your most caustic critic. Learn to do better by gauging what you did last.

Practice, practice, practice. Never rise to your feet without having given thought to what you are going to say.

When you use a prepared text, never, never, never speak those words without first making them your friends through constant and persistent attention.

Remember that an audience is composed of human beings subject to the same emotions you feel. Always treat them with the most loving care. Never permit yourself to think of them as mere breathing backboards for your words. Reach out to them; strive to let them know that you care about their feelings.

Speaking well is thinking clearly.

Speaking exceptionally well is thinking with exceptional clarity.

Finally, never allow yourself to believe, even for an instant, that you can succeed without thorough preparation. Not even the classiest professional is able to get away with that.

I can promise you only this: If you take to heart—and mind—what this small volume attempts to convey, the seeds of good speaking will be well planted.

You are beginning to be ready to speak up with confidence.